"Need a ride?" he called.

I ran around to the passenger side of the car in such a rush that I nearly spilled all my books.

"Thanks," I answered. *This was the closest I had ever been to Stu Shearin. Stu had lots of whatever it took. I could feel myself drawn like a moth to the flame already. He had crisp looking dark hair, china blue eyes and was tall enough to look kind of uncomfortable folded up in the little car.*

"How are things?" *he asked as we roared off. I noticed that he was wearing a china blue windbreaker that matched his eyes.*

"Great," *I answered.* "How about you?"

"This looks like a dead weekend." *He grinned at me.* "Why don't we take in a movie tomorrow night?"

Dear Readers:

Thank you for your many enthusiastic and helpful letters. In the months ahead we will be responding to your suggestions. Just as you have requested, we will be giving you more First Loves from the boy's point of view; and for you younger teens, younger characters. We will be featuring more contemporary, stronger heroines, and will be publishing, again in response to your wishes, more stories with bittersweet endings. Since most of you wanted to know more about our authors, from now on we will be including a short author's biography in the front of every First Love.

For our Book Club members we are publishing a monthly newsletter to keep you abreast of First Love plans and to share inside information about our authors and titles. These are just a few of the exciting ideas that First Love from Silhouette has in store for you.

Nancy Jackson
Senior Editor
Silhouette Books

HEAVENS
TO BITSY
Janice Harrell

First Love from Silhouette
Published by Silhouette Books New York
America's Publisher of Contemporary Romance

First Love from Silhouette by Janice Harrell

Puppy Love #67
Heavens to Bitsy #95

SILHOUETTE BOOKS, a Division of Simon & Schuster, Inc.
1230 Avenue of the Americas, New York, N.Y. 10020

ISBN: 0-671-53395-9

First Silhouette Books printing May, 1984

10 9 8 7 6 5 4 3 2 1

America's Publisher of Contemporary Romance

Printed in the U.S.A.

HEAVENS
TO BITSY

1

Everybody calls me Bitsy, which is bad enough, but my real name is even worse—Adele. I have often thought how different my life would have been if I had been named Desirée. A name like Desirée presents an image I could live with—dashing, daring, sensuous. I never wanted to actually *be* dashing, daring, and sensuous, you understand. I mean, how would I get my homework done? I knew I was basically fine the way I was, but I could see I needed a more zippy job of packaging. I knew of vicious-looking rock stars who secretly listened to Mozart and drank milk. I didn't see why I couldn't do the same sort of thing.

It was clear to me that I needed to do something about myself. Last fall Andy Lassiter took me to the Autumn Stomp, for instance, but when Georgia Allenby of the flashing eyes moved into town, Andy and I suddenly became just good friends, while Andy and Georgia became a hot item. Over the summer, to my delight, Georgia moved out of town again and took her bright eyes to Philadelphia, but still Andy showed no signs of beating a path to my door.

He knew I was still among the living because we were on the homecoming committee together, but that shortness of breath and tendency to trip over things that he had shown when Georgia was around had disappeared entirely. I just didn't radiate whatever it was that drew a boy to you like a moth to a flame.

It hit me forcibly on Claudia Oppenheimer's birthday. Claudia and I walked out of chemistry class at the same time, but while I faded anonymously into the woodwork, Claudia was greeted by a brass band. Honest. Three guys in gold-frogged uniforms were playing "Happy Birthday" on trombones. A clown handed Claudia a dozen red roses and turned a cartwheel. Then another clown began to hand out cake and ice cream. I do not exaggerate when I say this caused quite a stir in the halls of Riverdale High. Claudia Oppenheimer might not have had much in the way of a name, but you couldn't say she hadn't made an impact.

"Claudia's boy friend arranged it," Kathleen told me the next day. "He's rich," she added unnecessarily.

"He really must be boring to have to

overcompensate that way," I said. My father is a psychologist, and in my low moments I often find, to my horror, that I sound just like him.

"I think you're right," said Kathleen. "If there weren't something wrong with him, he'd just send a card like everyone else." It wasn't much comfort.

That night I went to Kathleen's house to work on the new me. I went to Kathleen's house because ever since we had moved into our ancient mausoleum of a house the summer before, anybody who stood still for three minutes there got a paintbrush put in their hand. Also, I didn't think I could stand it if my mother said something dumb like, "You look very sweet just the way you are, dear."

We settled down cozily in Kathleen's bedroom with a large stack of fashion magazines and began to thumb through them. I thought I had found my new image on page 34 of the September issue of *Vogue*, but Kathleen looked at the picture doubtfully. "I don't think it would look quite the same without that wind blowing," she said. When I looked at it closely, I saw what she meant. The woman did seem to be caught in a severe nor'easter. And when I gave it a close second look, I realized that was the way my hair looked already except that mine was combed.

Kathleen held out the August issue of *Mademoiselle*, regarding it with satisfaction. "Now *that's* a nice free look," she said.

"I don't think I'd get past the dress-code

committee," I replied, "in a blouse slit to my navel and no underwear."

"Well, you said you wanted a new look."

Twelve magazines later, we still had not made much progress.

"Maybe you should start out gradually," Kathleen suggested finally. "Try one small thing different, and if it works out all right, then you can add something else new. By December, there'll be a whole new you."

It made sense. We decided my first step would be my nails. Usually, when my nails get a half inch long, I trim them, because I like to be able to use my finger tips. But some sacrifices had to be made to reach my goal. I filed them to a pointy oval and painted them blood red. When I had finished, I felt I was getting somewhere. I thought they suggested that I was daring and faintly predatory.

Kathleen looked at them and shuddered. "Makes me think of vampires," she said.

"Not movie stars?"

"Well, maybe movie stars," she conceded.

The next afternoon, Andy and Lucinda Jackson and I stayed after school to try to get a head start on planning the homecoming floats. We were huddled over the yellow pages of the phone book, trying to figure out who would lend us trucks for the floats.

"Martin's Van Lines," read Lucinda. "Isn't that Tom Martin's father? We could ask him."

I put a blood-red finger on the listing. "Martin's Van Lines," I said thoughtfully.

"Yes, I think that's Tom's father." Had Andy noticed my nails? Were they working subliminally to suggest that he didn't really know me, that I had hidden depths?

"Are you okay, Bitsy?" asked Andy.

"What? Oh, I'm fine. I'm just thinking."

"Well, you seemed kind of out of it. What is that you've got on your nails?" He suppressed a shudder. "Reminds me of Dracula."

I put both my hands behind me hastily. "It's just nail polish," I said. Thank goodness it would come off.

By staying late to discuss trucks, I had, of course, missed the school bus. Andy grabbed his books and headed for the uptown library without offering to run me home. To be fair, I lived in exactly the opposite direction from the library, but on the other hand, it was a three-mile walk to my house. This was the sort of thing my parents could have spared me by letting me have a car, but they seemed to think the exercise was good for me. I picked up my books and started for home with a sigh.

I had walked only a few blocks when a red sports car pulled up on the opposite side of the road. I recognized the driver as Stu Shearin, captain of the tennis team and the swimming team and winner of the Latin Prize. I didn't exactly *know* him, but as a humble junior, I had admired his comet from afar as it blazed through Riverdale High.

"Need a ride?" he called.

I ran around to the passenger side of the car in such a rush I nearly spilled all my books.

"Thanks," I said. It was the closest I had ever been to Stu Shearin. After I sank into the bucket seat and buckled the seat belt, I surreptitiously slid my fingers under my chemistry book to hide my nails. The last thing I wanted was for him to look at me and shudder.

Stu had lots of whatever it took. I could feel myself drawn like a moth to a flame already. He had crisp-looking dark hair, china-blue eyes and was tall enough to look kind of uncomfortable folded up in the little car, as if his elbow might accidentally switch on the turn signal or something. I like tall men.

"How are things?" he asked as we roared off. I saw that he was wearing a blue windbreaker that matched his eyes. So what if his conversation wasn't sparkling?

"Great," I said. "How are things with you?"

"This looks like a dead weekend," he said. Then he grinned at me. "Why don't we take in a movie tomorrow night and cheer me up."

My chemistry book began to slide off my nails. I pushed it quickly back in place by hooking a thumb around it and pushing my stomach out to nudge it forward. "I'd love to," I said.

We were already pulling up in front of my house. Obviously, we had exceeded the speed limit. He reached over me to unlatch my door and throw it open. That knocked my chemistry book to the floor, and I had to pick it up in some confusion, but I was so thrilled when he brushed against me, I forgot all about my nails. He glanced curiously at the monster mansion where we lived but only said, "Pick you up at seven?"

"Great." I seemed to be saying "great" a lot. On the other hand, he must find me attractive. He had asked me out, hadn't he?

It was only later, inside the house, that I started having second thoughts. Of course, I thought, he only asked me out because he couldn't think of anyone else. What would he say when he found out about my Saturday night curfew? What would my parents say if they found out how fast he drove?

Picking my way through the paint cans that littered the hall, I made my way precariously to the hall mirror and looked at myself.

Now, Bitsy, I warned myself, don't be determined to milk all the misery you can out of this. Enjoy yourself for a change. I tousled my hair with one hand and let it drip over my face while I pouted my lips like a *Vogue* model. I could already see that I had a certain dash and glitter. If Andy had never noticed it, that was his loss.

I heard the back door open. "Bitsy?" Mom called.

It looked as though I would have to wait until later when I could get some peace and quiet to think about what it all meant, but I was sure it was a whole new chapter in my life, a whole new and definitely zippy chapter. "I'm coming!" I yelled.

A series of thuds told me that Mom had only made it as far as the door before dropping all her packages. Sure enough, when I got to the kitchen, I found her standing over a heap of paper bags, some of them split and some just overflowing. When I get to be forty, I expect I'll look just like Mom looks now. I have her brown eyes, her thick brown hair and her wispy, blow-away-in-a-strong-wind kind of figure, so it's easy to believe that with a few wrinkles and a sprinkling of gray hairs I could end up looking like her. What I can't believe is that I could ever end up being the kind of woman who stands over a heap of spilling paper bags with a smile on her face.

The thing with Mom is that she's a visionary. When she looks at those paper bags, she doesn't see paper bags the way I do; she sees their potential, how they'll turn into gourmet dinners and refinished furniture. I noticed that a roll of wallpaper was slowly rolling toward the refrigerator. The kitchen floor in our old house is not exactly level. I retrieved it and stood it on one end beside the paper bags.

"I've found the perfect wallpaper for the front bathroom," Mom said, glowing with satisfaction. "If we could just get the old wallpaper steamed off this weekend, I could start on it Monday." She looked at me speculatively.

"I'm going to be very busy this weekend," I

said quickly. "*Very* busy. For one thing, Monday is the deadline for the newspaper, and I still haven't finished either one of the articles Ronnie gave me. Then there's my chemistry homework, and also I have a date."

Mom bent over to unpack the bags and started stacking their contents on the kitchen counter. "A date? Why didn't you mention it before?" she said.

"Because I only got asked today."

"That seems like rather short notice," she said doubtfully, stacking cans of soup.

"It's just for a movie," I said.

"Who's the boy?" she asked. "Do I know him?"

"Stu Shearin," I said.

Mom's face cleared. "Oh, Dr. Shearin's son," she said. Doctor Shearin's office was in the same block of offices as Dad's before Dad moved his office into the third floor of our house, so she felt better right away. Mom has this strange idea that if she knows who a boy's parents are, he must be all right. "Well, even so," she said, "I'm sure you can spare a few hours to help me out. Getting this place fixed up is turning out to be more work than one person can possibly do."

"You're right," I said. "I think we ought to talk to Daddy about hiring someone to help you."

Mom raised an eyebrow at me. She seemed to have forgotten that when we bought the house, we had agreed that it was going to be her project, because Dad and I find it b-o-r-i-n-g. Personally, I had rather live in squalor the rest of my life than to spend my time wallpapering. And at the rate the remodeling was going, it looked as though I *was* going to be living in squalor the rest of my life.

"We'll have a family conference about it," she said. That didn't sound good. Now that my brother Jim was away at college, a family conference meant two against one. There was one comfort, though—Dad thought wallpaper was just as boring as I did. It was possible he might see it my way. I knew I had to stand my ground on this or I would have no time for a social life at all, even if Stu Shearin turned out to be crazy about me.

It wasn't until after supper that I was able to call up Kathleen to share the good news of Stu's asking me out. Calling her up isn't as easy as it sounds. Because she comes from a large and very disorganized family, it's like trying to get a message to the interior of some underdeveloped and overpopulated country. Sure enough, just as I had been afraid, Jamie, the three-year-old, answered the phone.

"Hewwo," he said.

"Hello, Jamie," I said cheerfully. "This is Bitsy. I want to talk to Kathleen."

Silence.

"Won't you please go get Kathleen for me, Jamie? Pretty please?"

More than one time, Jamie had gone off to play with his blocks at this point, leaving the phone off the hook, so I didn't stand on my pride. I *begged* him to get Kathleen. The phone receiver gave out loud clunking noises as he let his end fall to the floor, but finally Kathleen said, "Hello?"

"Is that you, Kathleen?" I said. "It's Bitsy."

"Why didn't you wait until the kids were in bed to call?" she asked. "You know how it is around here."

"I couldn't wait," I said. "You'll never guess who's asked me out. Stu Shearin!"

"Stu Shearin?" she said in disbelief.

Well, it was surprising, but I thought it wasn't very tactful of her to act as if she were going to die of shock.

"I didn't even know you knew him," she said. "Do you think it was the new fingernails that did it?"

"We—ll," I said. "I don't think so. I kind of kept them out of sight."

"I can't believe it," said Kathleen wonderingly. "You don't even know him."

"I suppose I'll *get* to know him after we spend some time together," I said with a slight edge to my voice. I thought your best friend was supposed to boost you up. Kathleen wasn't doing too good a job that night. She had almost got *me* wondering why Stu had asked me out.

Dad loomed up at my side. "Don't stay on the phone all night, Bitsy," he said. "I might be getting a call from a patient."

I had only just picked the phone up, but I knew it was hopeless to argue with Dad. He is always worried that some patient of his is going to commit suicide or something while our phone is tied up. "It looks like I gotta go now, Kathleen," I said. Between her impossible family and my impossible family, hope for further communication looked dim. "Maybe we'd better learn to talk to each other by tom-tom," I added bitterly.

I had the rest of the evening to think about going out with Stu, but thinking about it didn't make me more calm. Maybe Mom was right and it was short notice for a date. Did accepting at all make me look desperate? Maybe Kathleen was right and it was weird that he had asked me, me a lowly junior whom he doesn't even know. What could his motive be? Maybe he was into human sacrifice and I was his first victim. My thinking had started to get a bit wild, I noticed. Of course, I had gone places with boys before. One time I went to the class picnic with George Trakas. Another time Mickey Allen took me out for hamburgers. Then there was the time Andy Lassiter took me to the Autumn Stomp. But all those guys were guys I had known forever. Stu was entirely different. I had never been to nursery school with him. I had never played in his back yard. That was what made him so interesting. It was also what made me so nervous.

By the next morning, I had worked myself up into such a state that I bicycled over to Kathleen's house to get her opinion about what I should wear. Saturday morning was a good time to go to Kathleen's because then the wilder members of her family were hypnotized by television cartoons. Only Jamie, too young to be interested in cartoons, was at large. We barricaded the door of Kathleen's bedroom against him.

I perched on the stool of her dressing table. "I don't want to be overdressed," I explained. I added hastily, "And I don't want to try anything new, either." I still hadn't recovered from the disaster of the Dracula nails. "What do you think?" I went on urgently. "Have you ever noticed what sort of things his crowd wears?"

Kathleen gave it some thought. "Expensive . . . preppy," she judged.

That sounded discouraging. Since my family had started putting Jim through college and restoring the house at the same time, expensive was definitely not my style.

"Just wear the same thing you'd wear to the movies anytime," advised Kathleen. "It's not as if everybody he knows is a fashion plate. Doesn't Toni Alpert run around with that crowd? She looks like a rag bag."

I didn't think it would be safe to follow the example of Toni Alpert, since everybody knows she is an artist type and is expected to be eccentric.

"After all, he's not dating your wardrobe," said Kathleen.

"Sometimes you sound just like my mother," I said.

But she's right, I thought. It's the person that matters, after all, not the clothes. I was beginning to feel more calm when she said, "Imagine! Stu Shearin! *That's* really going to make Andy sit up and take notice."

My pulse made a frightened leap and took off running. Would I survive the evening?

But Kathleen was obviously not as transfixed as I was with the idea of my upcoming date, because she changed the subject. "If you want me to proof those articles Ronnie gave you," she said, "I could do it tonight."

"I haven't exactly finished them yet," I admitted. "Of course, I've got all tomorrow afternoon." I could see that if I should ever have a real social life, I would have to be a lot more efficient. I have quite a bit to do even without trotting off to the movies with Stu Shearin. Not to mention our crumbling mausoleum of a house, which was a career in itself. I sketched the latest in the house saga for Kathleen. "Now it's wallpapering the front bathroom," I said.

"I thought your mother was going to jack up the living-room floor next," she said.

"When Uncle Charlie stayed with us last weekend, Mom conned him into doing that. You know," I said, "what I need is for her to hire somebody to help her, somebody who'd come over in a regular way."

"Sounds like she needs a whole work crew," said Kathleen.

"Of course, it has to be somebody cheap," I went on. "That's what makes it tricky. My problem is that I'm the cheapest help around." I sighed. All of Mom's endless fixing up of that crumbling old house was really getting to me. It was okay for Mom because she loves to be always wallpapering, and it was okay for Dad because he can have his office in the old servants' quarters and enjoy the convenience, the quiet and everything. But what about me? Nobody thinks about me. I said gloomily, "You don't know what it's like to go to sleep at night to the sound of the clicking of mouse traps."

Kathleen lives in a sensible modern brick house, a bit crowded for her big family but definitely structurally sound and mouse free, so it was hard for her to sympathize with my troubles.

"It's bad," she admitted. "But you could be worse off. At least she's not embarrassing you in front of other people."

I could see her point. If Mom was going to do ridiculous things, at least I was lucky she was doing them in the privacy of our own home. I had a lot to be grateful for. Including, I reminded myself, that I was going out with Stu Shearin that night. Always assuming that I survived it, that is.

By the time Stu came to pick me up that evening, I had been both dreading it and looking forward to it so long that his showing up at the front door was a relief. Dad answered the door because before dinner part of the ceiling of the ballroom had come down on Mom's head, showering her with plaster and ancient mouse skeletons. She had a Band-Aid on her nose and was upstairs shampooing her hair for the third time. I figured I was lucky to have at least one presentable parent. Dad greeted Stu cordially, while Stu sneaked looks around the room. Fortunately, the library, the room we were standing in, was the first place that had been restored, so it looked perfectly clean and in good repair, even though old-fashioned. The molding in the library, for example, is all full of curlicues, like icing on a wedding cake, and the room actually has a beaded chandelier. Naturally, Stu couldn't take his eyes off it all. People around here, if they want luxuries, get things like outdoor decks, barbecues or sauna baths—something useful. Not us. We get curlicues and beaded chandeliers. I had privately vowed that if I ever grew up and got out of this place, it was going to be stainless steel and plate glass forever for me.

There was a brief pause while Stu tried to think of something nice to say. "This is really an interesting old house," he managed finally.

"My wife is restoring it bit by bit," said Dad. "Here, let me show you something rather unusual."

My toes curled in my shoes. Dad was losing no time showing off the only thing in the whole house he really liked. It was harmless enough, I guess, but I had no desire to be known as the girl with the kooky house. I've heard girls complain about being upstaged by their mothers when a boy comes over, but how much more humiliating to be upstaged by a house.

Dad strode over to the mantelpiece and grabbed hold of the carved pineapple on the molding, then pulled on it. Stu stood there with his mouth open as the wall-to-ceiling bookcase on the east wall slowly swung open like a door.

"Good grief," he said. "It's a secret door."

Dad beamed. It had cost a lot to have the thing put into working order, and still sometimes the pineapple would come off in his hand instead of opening the secret cabinet, so he was very pleased it had worked.

Stu peered into the shelves behind the secret door. "But it doesn't lead anyplace," he said. "There are just these shelves."

I sat down on the arm of Dad's leather chair, resigned to being late to the movie. "Dad thinks that was just old Judge Moran's liquor cabinet," I explained. "It doesn't actually go anywhere."

"Well, I'll be darned," said Stu wonderingly, looking back and forth from the movable pineapple to the concealed shelves. "I wonder how it works."

Of course, Dad didn't have the faintest idea how it worked and wouldn't have understood if anybody had told him. He is strictly nonmechanical, so Stu got nowhere with his questions about gears. You could see that if it had been Stu's house, splinters of wood would soon have been flying all over the place as he tore the wall apart to find the mechanism.

"The man to talk to would be Adam Winter, the cabinetmaker," Dad said finally. "He's the one who put it in order for us." He glanced at his watch. "You kids had better be getting on to the movie or you're going to be late."

It was obvious that Stu didn't feel rushed to get there on time, but then he knew what

Dad didn't—that he was going to speed the whole way there.

Shortly, we were zooming away in the little red car. "That's some house you have there," said Stu. It was a hard remark to disagree with. Also, I had to admit, the house was a good conversational topic. I certainly wasn't going to have to fall back on "Read any good books lately?" with Judge Moran's crazy house at hand to discuss.

"Mom loves it," I said. "She spends hours at the library doing research to figure out exactly what it looked like when it was first built. Then she spends more hours looking for wallpaper authentic at the time it was built—that sort of thing." I told him about the ballroom upstairs, which had so many possibilities that Mom preferred thinking about the possibilities to actually doing anything with it. I told him about the bathtubs, which had the plumbers in stitches. I heaved a sigh. "One thing about living in a house like that," I said, "it makes you realize how much civilization has progressed in the past hundred years."

As we rounded a sharp corner at forty, I dug my fingernails into the armrest. "What'll it be?" said Stu. *"Return of the Bloodsuckers or Honeybunch Goes to Summer Camp."* I looked startled. "Just kidding," he explained hastily.

We pulled up to the theater without a minute to spare and ran up to the ticket window. Stu quickly slapped the money down at the ticket window, and we slipped inside. I got the feeling he always did things at a dead run and wasn't a bit rattled by the rush. Soon we were sitting side by side in a dark theater amid a hundred other anonymous heads, and I was thinking that although I had told Kathleen I expected to get to know Stu, a movie was not really a very good place to get to know somebody. I mean, it could have been the bloodsucker himself in the next seat for all the talking I got to do. Also, it turned out to be a very depressing movie.

When the houselights finally came on, Stu took my hand and led me out through the crowd, cutting in and out of slower-moving people like a quarter horse. Once we got outside, I buttoned my jacket against the autumn air and put my hands in my pockets to keep them warm.

"Good movie," commented Stu.

"It must have been," I said, shivering. "It sure made you feel like you wish you were dead."

Stu was again wearing his blue windbreaker and looked great. I had the uncomfortable feeling that my nose was red.

"Could you eat something?" he said.

I said I could always eat something, so we got in the car and headed toward Mamma Carabanini's Pizza Place, which is right next to our shopping mall and usually crowded with kids. After we walked into the steamy air of the place, for a second we stood together at the lighted counter, both of us trying to peer into the dark interior where the jukebox was playing.

"Stu!" somebody called.

Stu's face broke into a smile, and he guided me in the direction of the familiar voice, where we found a bunch of kids wedged into a corner booth. Miraculously, they made room for us. Toni Alpert was squeezed in right next to me. She didn't look like a rag bag exactly. She looked more like a gypsy in deep mourning—long gold earrings and everything else layers of black ruffles. On anybody else it would look pretty silly, but she managed to carry it off. She had a sweet face and long crinkly hair that was pulled back in a black ribbon.

I had to be introduced to everybody. I recognized most of their faces, but naturally nobody recognized mine. There was Harlan O'Brian, our star fullback, taking up two places at the booth with his bulk. Michael Cowder, president of the student body, was sitting in a corner looking as earnest and responsible as anyone can look eating pizza. Then there was Toni, in her gypsy outfit, Marian Sweeney, of the student government, Stu, and me. Me? What was I doing there? I fingered the grated cheese shaker nervously to keep from biting my nails.

"Are you pretty hungry, Bitsy?" said Stu.

"Not very," I said in a small voice.

"Then maybe we'll just get the twelve-inch pizza."

He slid away from the table and walked over to the lighted counter at the entrance to put in our order.

Now I was alone with all these people. Also, they were looking at me.

"Are you new in town, Bitsy?" asked Marian kindly.

Now here was one of those occasions where a name like Bitsy let you down. It wasn't just that it lacked glamour. It even lacked dignity.

"No," I said, "I'm just inconspicuous."

I could see they were thinking, What is this girl doing here? She isn't wildly gorgeous, and she isn't famous like us. She is an impostor. Soon Stu was making his way past the salad bar, coming back. I was really glad to see him. At least he was a friendly face.

Michael Cowder leaned toward me from his corner, accidentally getting mozzarella on his elbow. I watched it stretching stringily from table to elbow, fascinated. "What do you like to do?" he asked me.

Stu slid into the booth. He looked happy, as if he'd been having the best time in the world ordering a small mushroom and pepperoni pizza. He heard what Michael was asking me and put in, "Bitsy writes features for the *Clarion*."

Michael looked relieved. You had the idea that in his mind people didn't have personalities, just achievements.

Toni crinkled up her eyes in a smile. "Sometimes they're very funny," she said softly.

"Thank you," I said.

I thought for a minute she was going to have to explain what "funny" was to Michael, who had permanent serious creases between his brows.

The only light in the gloom of the booth was cast by candle, but when I got used to the dark, I could make people out pretty well. It looked as though Kathleen had been right when she said their style was mostly expensive and preppy, but Harlan the hulk was wearing what looked like the oldest sweatshirt in the world over some kind of sweater, and then there was Toni in the black flounces, so I didn't feel I came off too badly in my best sweater and skirt.

Stu began treating everyone to a highly colored account of Mrs. Hill's French class. Mrs. Hill is more than a little senile, and everybody but the administration knows it. She is likely to say things that are unconsciously funny, like "I'd quit teaching if I got to the point I couldn't control my class." Meanwhile kids are crawling in and out the windows and picnicking in the aisles without her noticing it. It was because Mrs. Hill taught French that I had decided to take Spanish.

"Are you taking her course?" Michael asked Stu incredulously.

Stu looked at him with his guileless blue eyes. "I got permission to sit in on it during my study hall," he explained. "I didn't want to miss the experience."

I could see that it would be funny in a

black-humor sort of way, but I have too much imagination to get a kick out of that sort of thing. After all, what's the difference between Mrs. Hill and the rest of us? Just fifty years, give or take a decade.

I was glad to see the waitress bringing our pizza. It meant I had something to do with my hands and mouth. Sitting squeezed in a pizza booth with nothing to do but look intelligent while other people talk can wear a person down. I picked up a pizza slice and nibbled tentatively at the corner of it, trying to analyze how I felt. My father says that if you analyze how you feel, you'll immediately feel better. I realized that I felt that I was out of my league. These people had known each other forever and had running jokes that probably went years back. I didn't fit in at all. Once I had figured that out, I felt better. It wasn't that anything was wrong with me, after all. I was just in the wrong place.

Just as I had come to this conclusion, in came Andy Lassiter—with a girl. I didn't know her, but I recognized right away a certain resemblance that she had to Andy's old girl friend Georgia. Her hair wasn't the same color, her eyes were different, and she was thinner, but there was something about the way she paused at the lighted counter as if she were waiting for applause that reminded me of Georgia. Andy stood beside her, peering into the dark room, the way people do when they first come in, looking very solid, dependable and predictable, with his neatly combed hair. I stifled a sigh. If I had managed to cook up the kind of sizzle that girl had, I would have been standing there by Andy's side where I obviously belonged instead of squirming here in this booth, being totally out of my league.

I remembered what Kathleen had said about how, when Andy saw that I had gone out with Stu, he would really sit up and take notice. I wished I could think of some way to make Andy see that I was with Stu that night. It was too bad that the pizza place had the lighting effects of your average bat cave.

But then suddenly things went my way. Stu said, "I want something else to drink. Anybody else want a soft drink?" Everybody did, and when Stu got up to go get the drinks, he strode right past Andy and his girl, so naturally Andy noticed him. And when he came back to the table carrying six tall cups of cold drinks, Andy's eyes followed him the whole way. *Anybody* would have noticed him because he carried them up over his head with one hand, his dark brows straight in concentration but with a look on his face as if he might laugh and dump them all. When he got as far as the salad bar, he wheeled around on one toe, still keeping the drinks aloft, and returned to our booth without spilling a drop. "My coordination is legendary," he said modestly as he slid in.

"You'd have felt pretty silly if you'd spilled them all," said Marian Sweeney.

Stu grinned. "I'd have gotten pretty wet, anyway."

I saw Andy's double take as he noticed that

I was sitting in the same booth with all those legendary seniors. I felt a little glow of pleasure. This might do the trick where my dragon-lady nail polish had failed. Maybe some of the glamour of Stu's gang would reflect on me. Only it was going to have to work fast, since it seemed pretty unlikely that Stu would ever ask me out again.

After he distributed the soft drinks, Stu waved his pizza in the air and began, "There once was a teacher named Hilly."

Harlan rolled his eyes and groaned. He obviously had a larynx as big as the rest of him, because when he groaned, it sounded like a Mack truck dying. "Not that again," he rumbled.

Beside me, Toni piped in, "Who acted exceedingly silly."

I began to see that it was a limerick game. Stu and Toni had already come up with the first two lines: "There once was a teacher named Hilly, / Who acted exceedingly silly." Now the rest of us were supposed to finish it.

The creases between Michael's brows deepened as he gave the matter serious thought. "You two have done the easy part," he protested, but he finally volunteered, "She wasn't too bright."

Stu quickly matched his line with "And her hair was a sight."

There was a silence. Obviously, limericks were not Marian Sweeney's thing. Her face was completely blank. Fascinated, I put my pizza slice down and said, "And her class ran around willy-nilly."

Then everybody looked at me, naturally, and I blushed all over.

"Stu likes to play that game," Toni explained to me, "because he's the only one who's any good at it."

"Not true," protested Stu. "I brought Bitsy tonight, and she's good at it."

He patted my hand.

Stu and Harlan started an argument over which sport took the most self-discipline, tennis or football. I had the feeling Harlan was the only one taking it seriously. While they were busy arguing, it hit me that it was odd Stu knew I wrote features for the school newspaper. The newspaper staff aren't exactly celebrities around school. In fact, the way people act, you would think the stuff wrote itself. The *Clarion* staff doesn't get any of this "Great game last night" that the football players get. I had decided that most people were completely unable to connect the written word with the person who wrote it. Or, an even more depressing thought, writing looks so easy they think it's not worth mentioning. Anyway, whatever the reason, I've written pounds of features for the paper, but what Toni and Stu had said that night was the first notice anybody had taken of it. Had Stu actually read my articles and gone to the trouble to find out who I was? That would be even stranger than the idea that he had asked me out on a crazy whim.

I realized that I liked Stu. I mean, he might have an overblown sense of humor, too much energy, and the driving habits of a maniac, but there was something about him you had to like. It was too bad that I felt so uncomfortable around his friends.

It seemed as if I sat for a long time squeezed in at that booth. I had plenty of chance to notice Andy, sitting at a table near the salad bar with his girl. Every now and then, I would look over that way, and from the way they acted, I guessed they didn't know each other very well. Obviously, Andy was stealing some looks at our table, too, because at one unnerving moment, our eyes met. I gave him an uncertain smile and a little wave. He knocked over his salt shaker. He definitely looked rattled, but whether it was from a sudden interest in me or just embarrassment at his being caught looking at us was hard to say.

A couple of minutes later, Stu asked, "Are you asleep, Bitsy?"

"Uh, no," I said. "Just thinking."

To my relief, he didn't ask me what I was thinking about. "I gotta get Bitsy home, folks," he said. "She's got a midnight curfew."

Michael looked at his watch and said, "Aren't you cutting it kind of close?"

"Oh, we'll make it," said Stu easily.

Everybody laughed. Obviously, these kids had ridden with him before.

After the steamy atmosphere of the pizza parlor, it seemed even chillier outside than before as we made our way to the little sports car. The moon was very clear, the way it gets in cold weather. You could make out the shadows of the mountains and craters on it. I scrunched myself up in the little red car, doing my best to keep myself decently covered as I got in, no easy thing.

"It came with a shoehorn," Stu said soberly as he got in, "but I lost it."

He stepped on the accelerator. "You can go faster in a car like this one," he explained to me, "because you have better control. Notice how there's nothing spongy about this steering." I felt faint as he demonstrated the responsive steering of the car. Let's face it, physically, I am a coward. By going fifty in a thirty-five-mile zone, he managed to easily get me home in time for my curfew. I was very glad to get my feet on solid ground again when we got to my house.

Stu walked me up to the door, but he didn't kiss me good night. I had mixed feelings about that. I never expected to see him again, but he was definitely the most attractive guy I had ever met.

As I stepped into the hall and closed the door behind me, I found myself thinking that although I might not yet be a senior, I had aged a year that night between being petrified of Stu's driving and being afraid of his high-flown friends. Also, I was feeling a little punchy from having eaten all that pizza, and my mind was reeling with questions. What was glamour, anyway? It was what I was going to have to get in order to attract Andy, that's what. Also, it was what Stu's crowd already had, but on them it just seemed to make me feel uncomfortable. Was it my problem? Maybe I was too easily impressed. What a night! It certainly hadn't been the way I had imagined.

"Bitsy?" Mom called from the kitchen.

I went into the kitchen and found Mom and Dad drinking cocoa at the kitchen table. I flopped down next to them in a chair. They were wearing thick bathrobes, since our kitchen is drafty, and I figured they had waited up for me to ask me about Stu. But to my surprise, they seemed to have forgotten he existed.

"Your mother has decided the house is haunted," said Dad.

I couldn't help it. I smiled.

"Really, Bitsy," Mom said earnestly. "One of the upstairs toilets has started flushing mysteriously when no one is around."

This time I didn't even try to control myself. I grinned widely. I had been under a lot of strain all evening, and I thought this definitely came under the heading of comic relief.

"But seriously," she said. "And I haven't mentioned this before," she went on, lowering her voice, "but mysterious figures have been appearing in my checkbook."

This time Dad smiled. "Look here, sweetheart, your checkbook has always been a mystery."

"But Eliot, there are figures in there that I never put there."

I may look like my mother, but I think like my father. We looked at each other and grinned.

"Laugh if you like," said Mom, "but explain the flushing toilet."

"Some mechanical malfunction," said Dad airily, with the reasoning of someone who naturally groups mechanics with the occult.

"Water leak," I suggested.

"All right," said Mom, "but if some pale apparition comes wafting through your bedroom tonight, don't blame me."

"How was your date, 'Punkin'?" Dad asked.

"Okay, I guess. Stu is nice, but I don't fit in with his crowd."

Mom and Dad instantly looked alert. I could see they were afraid Stu's crowd was the criminal set, so I quickly added, "You know, they're all the school leaders, that type."

That sounded harmless enough, so Mom and Dad resumed their usual slumps.

"Well, maybe the movie was good, anyway," said Mom, stifling a yawn.

I thought about it. "No," I said. "The movie was awful, too."

Dad pushed his chair back from the table and got up. "Can't win 'em all," he said.

That was very true, I thought as I trudged upstairs to my bedroom. But the problem was that I didn't seem to be winning any of them. I thought back nostalgically to the Autumn Stomp a year before. Andy had acted the whole time as if his collar were too tight, but I had been calm and happy. Back then I was full of confidence. Not like now.

After an evening with Stu and company, what I had was a complete lack of confidence.

In my room, I dressed for bed, feeling the cold, uneven floorboards under my toes. It was lucky Dad had insisted on putting in central heating, even though Mom said it might warp the paneling. Even as it was, the central heating was losing the battle with the drafts. I hated to think what it would have been like if we depended on fireplaces. A draft moved my white curtains a bit, and I jumped. An interesting example of what Dad called the power of the unconscious. I might laugh at Mom's ghost, but obviously my unconscious believed in it.

I guessed Stu must be back to his own house by now. I imagined his telling his parents, "Yeah, I took this unknown junior to the movies. What a bust."

Of course, there was still the chance the evening might not be a total loss. Maybe now that Andy had seen me in stellar company, he would see my true value.

Lucky for me, I never have trouble falling asleep, because thoughts like mine would have kept an insomniac awake for a week.

3

Monday afternoon, Ronnie Platt, our school newspaper editor, was having a few words with his staff. Ronnie is a short, ugly guy with ears that stick out and hair as straight as uncooked spaghetti. I would expect somebody who looked like Ronnie to have a nature humbled and sweetened by the adversity of being ugly, but he doesn't. When the pencil he wears stuck over one ear begins to wobble and his black eyes start to bore into you, you know you're really going to get it. Sylvia Blackburn had just gotten a few choice words from him on the subject of turning her copy in handwritten and half finished, and she was sitting beside me, shaking like a leaf.

"Now Ronnie," said Mrs. Greenbaum, our

adviser, "I'm sure Sylvia will do better next time."

No one paid the slightest attention to Mrs. Greenbaum. We all knew that it was Ronnie who ran the paper.

Ronnie gave Sylvia a dark glance. "It's a good thing there are people here I can count on," he said, patting me on the shoulder. "People like Bitsy here, whose copy is always perfect."

I leaned on one hand so I could surreptitiously prop my eyelid open with my finger. Mom had needed Dad's and my help Sunday afternoon buttressing the rest of the ballroom ceiling to prevent its further collapse, and getting my copy in on time had meant staying up until two.

"All I ask," said Ronnie sweetly, "is that if you can't type it up yourself, get it finished in time to hand to the typists on Thursday. Is that too much to ask?"

We all gathered our books and fled.

"I may quit the newspaper," said Sylvia tearfully when we got out in the hall.

"Oh, it'll blow over," I said. "Don't let Ronnie get to you." I asked curiously, "What happened that you didn't get your stuff finished?"

"I had a date," said Sylvia. "What does Ronnie expect? That the whole world will come to a screeching stop so I can write some dumb interview with the new math teacher? There are other things in life, you know."

I saw I had been a little hasty in saying it

would blow over. If Sylvia kept up that attitude, Ronnie might kill her. "If you're too busy, maybe you ought to quit, after all," I said.

"I would in a snap," said Sylvia, "but Allie Smith is leaving, and there's going to have to be a new feature editor." She sniffled. "I thought I might have a shot at it."

Sylvia knew she couldn't count on Ronnie's good opinion of her. She must be banking on the fact that she was the only senior on the staff whose name wasn't on the masthead. On our paper, it's normally the seniors who get the glory of being editors.

"You'll have to decide for yourself," I said, "whether that's worth having Ronnie bawl you out every staff meeting." I was starting to sound like my father again, but it had hit me that when Allie left, I might have a shot at that job myself.

I saw Kathleen at lunch time. She pulled up a chair beside me and unpacked her bologna sandwich. In a family as big as Kathleen's, lunch money can be a major expense, so everybody packs their own. "How did it go?" she whispered.

"What?" I said. I was so busy thinking how I'd like to be feature editor that I didn't see what she was talking about.

"The date with Stu!" she said impatiently. "It was all you could talk about a couple of days ago."

I glanced around me nervously. I didn't want to discuss my private life in the middle of the cafeteria.

"I don't expect I'll be hearing from him again," I said.

Kathleen looked attentive.

"I felt so uncomfortable around his friends," I said.

Kathleen bit into her bologna. "All that glitters is not gold," she said sagely.

I didn't feel that quite summed it up. "They're all right," I said. "But I'm just not in that class."

I thought it would have showed more tact on Kathleen's part if she had disagreed, but she just peacefully chewed her bologna.

That night I went to bed at nine. I was tired. But no sooner had I drifted off than Mom came in my bedroom and woke me up. "Phone call for you, Bitsy," she said. I quickly jumped up and groped for my bedroom slippers. "I didn't think you'd mind being woken up," she said, smiling.

It was Stu. "How would you like to go out for hamburgers Friday night?" he said. "This is the last week you can get the Dead-eye Dick secret decoder with cheeseburger and fries."

"Sounds like fun," I said.

"Pick you up at seven?" he said.

I hung up the phone in a trance. Weird. Stu had asked me out again. Somehow, in a way, it puzzled me more than the first time. The first time he asked me out, he might as well have been a creature from another planet as far as I was concerned. He wasn't a person to me. He was glamour, romance, adventure.

But now that I saw what he was like, I realized that he and I just didn't make a good match. I was surprised he hadn't noticed it, too.

Kathleen came over to my house the next afternoon to do trig. She wanted to go upstairs and see where the ceiling had collapsed. It seemed like a strange request to me, but I humored her. "Okay," I said. "We can go up now. Mom's up there now with the men from Brandon's."

We could hear Mr. Brandon talking as we came up the steps. "Lady, this is the twentieth century," he was saying. "There ain't no such thing as a plasterer. You want a drywall man."

Kathleen and I peered in the ballroom door.

"Hi, girls," said Mom brightly. "Have you gotten yourselves some cookies and milk?" When she got tense Mom tended to forget that I wasn't still six.

"I say lower the ceiling," said Mr. Brandon, "and cut your heating bills."

"Sell this house," I muttered, "and *really* cut your heating bills."

"It's an awful big room," Kathleen said, peering through the door with awe. "What are you going to do with it?"

I looked at the heaps of fallen plaster along the north wall. "Mom is still considering the possibilities," I said. I finally managed to drag Kathleen away.

"I think some cookies *would* be nice,"

Kathleen said as we went downstairs, so we ended up settling in the kitchen with cookies and milk, after all.

"Boy, what my family could do with all this space," said Kathleen, looking around the kitchen.

"Believe me, you don't want it," I said. "Listen, Kathleen. You'll never guess what's happened. Last night, Stu called and asked me out again."

Kathleen has this soft, wavy brown hair that she wears pulled away from her face with a barrette, and unlike me, she normally looks very calm and contented, but just then I saw a twinge of sadness flash across her face. "Gee," she said. "Pretty soon people may be calling you 'Stu's girl.'"

"Well . . . maybe," I said.

"I hope you'll still have time for your old friends," said Kathleen mournfully.

It struck me that Kathleen looked a lot like a cocker spaniel. "Of course I'll always have time for my old friends," I said. "I'm not going away to another planet. I'm just going out with a boy."

"You'd be surprised how that changes people," said Kathleen glumly.

Friday night, Stu came by to pick me up for hamburgers. As usual, he took off from our house as if he were trying to get the car into orbit. I wished he would wait until we got out of sight of the house before he hit the accelerator. I was afraid Dad might look out the window some evening as we were leaving. I knew Dad had strong opinions about reckless drivers. As for me, I could hardly put together a sensible sentence until we got out of the car and I had my feet on solid ground again.

"You don't like going fast, do you?" Stu said as he opened the door to the Burger Place for me.

"Not really," I admitted in the understatement of the year.

"I love it," he purred. "It makes me feel free." We joined the line inside, which was heavily populated with kids under ten, eager for the secret decoder. I noticed that Stu always held his head high, the way horses and dancers do, as if he were looking at some far horizon. Maybe that was why you noticed so much the curve of his jaw. He turned to look at the menu board. "You only get the secret decoder with the Funtime Meal," he explained. "I hope you like cheeseburgers."

I could see that Stu really *wanted* that secret decoder.

He turned back toward me. "Look, I'm sorry if my driving makes you nervous," he said. "When it gets too fast for you, just tell me to cool it. Sometimes I don't think."

I thought that was more than generous of him, since I could see how much he longed to floor the accelerator, but I couldn't imagine myself sitting in the passenger's seat timidly chirping, "Too fast—too fast." I would just have to suffer.

Soon we gathered up our Funtime Meals and took them on trays to a booth. We sat on opposite sides of the table, unwrapping our cheeseburgers, but Stu stretched out one long leg and propped his foot on the seat on my side. It was amazing how distracting it was to have his leg there right next to me.

I tried to concentrate on my secret decoder. You put on these little cardboard glasses with blue cellophane lenses, and suddenly you could read the secret message on your cheeseburger package.

"I'll be darned," said Stu. "I wonder who thinks these things up."

"They probably have a roomful of people who do nothing but sail paper airplanes at each other all day and think things up."

"Now there's a job I could love," said Stu.

"What would you want if you could have three wishes," I said suddenly. I was determined to get to know him.

"Uh, world peace . . . justice . . ."

"No, no, I mean wishes for yourself."

"Oh, well, a Maserati, to always have a good time, and—oh, I give up." He grinned. "What would yours be?"

"Easy. Gain ten pounds, be feature editor and live in a plain brick house."

"But you don't need to gain ten pounds, Bitsy," he said, looking me over. "You're perfect just the way you are."

That sort of remark makes you feel like you're being buttered up. I squirmed. "You won't deny I could use the brick house, though, will you?" I said.

"I like your house," he said.

This conversation wasn't turning out at all the way I had planned. Instead of getting to know what Stu was really like, I had ended up talking about the house—again.

Stu bit into his cheeseburger while I filled him in on the mice and the need for wallpapering, painting and refinishing. I did not mention the ghost, since if anybody is going to laugh at my mother, I want it to be just me.

"What you need is some teenaged boy to help your mother out," he said. "Someone who's handy."

"Like you, you mean?"

"Not me," he said. "Someone who can use a little extra money."

Well, obviously, when I thought about it. People didn't usually drive their sports cars to their odd jobs, although to hear Dad talk, you might think the plumbers were supporting a sports-car habit.

"It's an idea," I said, picking up a french fry. "Lots of kids our age could use some extra spending money." In fact, when I thought about it, just about everybody I knew figured they could use some extra money except for Stu. "Do you have any brothers or sisters?" I asked him suddenly.

He grinned. "I know what you're thinking," he said. "You're thinking I'm so spoiled I must be an only child."

I hoped I wasn't blushing guiltily, because that had been exactly what I was thinking.

"Not at all," I said stiffly. "I'm only trying to get to know you."

"Well, the answer is yes. I have a brother, Brian, aged thirteen, and a sister, Sara, aged ten."

"Are they like you?" I said with real curiosity.

"Jeez, no. They're real nice kids."

Stu was not an easy person to get to know. But one thing this date with him did have over our last one—at least I ended up with a neat secret decoder.

The next week, I heard from Stu again. He asked me to go with him to a party at Michael Cowder's. At first, it sounded like almost a contradiction in terms. It was hard to imagine Michael having fun. What were we all going to do? Sit around reading *Robert's Rules of Order?* But whatever the party was like, it was definitely another date with Stu. I gave the matter some serious thought while I painted my toenails that night. Stu's girl. Was that what I wanted to be?

When I talked about this to Kathleen later on, she thought it was funny. "A couple of weeks ago," she said, "you were acting like Stu was the chance of a lifetime."

I thought about that. "It looked better from a distance," I said. "Now you take somebody like Andy. I understand Andy. I've known him all my life. With somebody like Andy, you know where you are."

"Ignored is where you are," said Kathleen.

"I never feel like I really know what Stu is thinking," I complained. "And whatever happened to your idea that Andy was going to be impressed by my going out with Stu and really start to notice me?"

"Well," said Kathleen reasonably, "you can't expect him to move in on Stu's girl, can you? He knows when he's outclassed."

I thought about that for a minute. It didn't seem fair. Andy didn't notice me until I went out with Stu, but as long as I was going out with Stu, he wouldn't pay any attention to me. "Andy is an idiot," I said crossly.

"I thought you liked Andy," said Kathleen in surprise.

Michael Cowder's party wasn't as grim as I expected. Michael's father barbecued chicken in the back yard. Since my new tweed jacket turned out to be pretty thin, Stu and I ended up eating our chicken by the fire in the family room. When it got colder, the others came inside, too, but at first we had the fire to ourselves.

I found out that the reason Stu's father kept him so plentifully supplied with spending money and cars was because of his good grades. "He expects me to go to medical school," Stu said.

"Aren't you?" I asked.

"It's too soon to say," Stu said vaguely.

Maybe for some people, I thought, but not in a family like Stu's. "Wasn't your grandfather a doctor, too?" I asked. I seemed to remember people talking about old Doctor Shearin.

Stu nodded. "Brain surgeon. He was still a good brain surgeon right into his sixties, but when he started to forget people's names . . ." He paused delicately.

"I can see how that would shake the patients' confidence," I agreed. "Don't you think you'll probably end up being a doctor, too?" I asked.

Stu's eyes took on that guileless look that I now knew to suspect. "I might not be able to get into medical school," he said.

"Don't you *want* to be a doctor?" I said. I had the idea that everybody wanted to be a doctor. Not me, of course, but then blood makes me feel faint.

"Well," said Stu, "look at my father."

I tried to remember Dr. Shearin from the few times I'd seen him, a bald man with a big stomach, as I remembered. Looking at him might make you think Stu was adopted, but I didn't see that it led you to any conclusions about studying medicine. I had never heard anyone say that medical school made you fat and bald.

"You know, the red blotches at his neck when he gets excited? High blood pressure," Stu said, shaking his head gravely. "I wouldn't want to end up like that."

"You have to consider your health," I agreed, biting into a chicken leg. "But you just don't want to be a doctor, do you?"

"What do you think? Medicine, medicine, medicine," he said. "It's all I hear about day and night. Is your father always talking about his work?"

He looked more than usually interested, but then I am used to people having a morbid interest in Dad's work. They seem to imagine he can read people's minds or something. Nobody sees that being a psychologist is just like being a dentist or anything else. "No," I said, "he never talks about his work. I mean, you could go to Dad to complain about your hangnails, and he'd be roasted over hot coals before he'd breathe a word of it. You wouldn't believe what a big deal confidentiality is around our house."

Stu looked so interested that for a minute I thought maybe he was thinking of "seeking help," as they say. Then it occurred to me that he was probably just thinking about careers a lot because he was a senior. Maybe he thought a psychologist was less likely to end up with high blood pressure than a physician.

"But having his office right in your house and everything," he insisted, "don't you know a lot of what goes on?"

"Might as well be in another country," I said. "All the shrubbery, the separate outside staircase and so on. If it weren't for that, Dad would never have moved the office to the house. Of course, he needed a lot more room than he had in his old office. Now he has a play-therapy room and all. But he never would have moved if our house hadn't been almost uptown and if the office setup hadn't been really private. You wouldn't be-

51

lieve how uptight people are about going to see a psychologist. Dad says the big problem with getting an office is that it has to be inconspicuous enough so that no one will be seen coming there and conspicuous enough that no one will have to ask directions, because nobody is going to be willing to ask directions, you can bet on that. You aren't thinking about becoming a psychologist, are you?"

"It's an idea," said Stu.

I had been so interested in what we were talking about that I hadn't even realized we were sitting knee to knee by the fire until Michael came in and looked embarrassed. I guess he thought he was breaking up a romantic tête-à-tête.

"We're moving inside," he said apologetically. "It's getting really cold out there."

People started streaming in, carrying plates and hot coffee. Toni sat down at the piano and started playing. Soon people bunched up around her, singing, trying to follow the words and music in the dim light. We all sang out the choruses nice and strong, but the verses were sort of scraggly. I really like to sing. I mean, I like to sing anything, even "The Star Spangled Banner," so for me it was fun. But something happened that took my attention away from the music. Toni looked up at Stu and smiled. It doesn't sound like much, but it was then that I realized Toni really went for Stu in a big way.

I thought about that later that night when

Stu and I were driving home. You might even say I was lost in thought, because it came as a complete surprise to me when I realized that Stu had pulled over to the side of the road and parked. My fingers felt cold all of a sudden. This is it, I thought. This is where he sprouts horns and tail and produces a pitchfork from the glove compartment. This is where I get to take the dimes out of my loafers and call Dad to come get me.

"The trouble with these parties," Stu said, "is that you don't really get much chance to talk."

I didn't say anything. I was saving my breath for running.

Stu looked at me curiously. The light from the street lamp shone on his face, casting his eyes into shadow, but so far no sign of horns. He looked, in fact, sort of friendly. "You're a hard person to get to know, Bitsy," he said finally.

He had it all wrong. *He* was the one who was hard to get to know.

"You never talk about yourself," he went on. "You're always talking about that blinking house."

That was a serious accusation, and I wasn't sure I could deny it.

"What are you thinking right now?" he said.

I was actually thinking about the house and how it was ruining my life, but of course I couldn't say that. "I was wondering how you ever happened to ask me out," I said. "There's Toni . . ." My voice trailed off.

Stu looked uncomfortable. "Well, I've known Toni my whole life," he said. "Of course, she's a very nice girl—"

"But you wanted romance, adventure, glamour."

Stu grinned. "Well, something different, anyway. I read your stuff in the paper, and I thought it would be fun to get to know you." Even in the dim light, I could see his impish look appearing. "Then there's your hair," he said. "I'm crazy about your hair."

He reached over and started running his fingers through it.

"I'm getting really cold," I said. "I think we'd better go on."

"Cold?" he grinned. "I can fix that."

Fortunately, the bucket seats really limited his maneuverability. I pushed him away. "Really," I said firmly.

He agreeably switched on the ignition and pulled the car out onto the street.

"Don't you ever feel embarrassed, uncomfortable, like your collar is too tight or something?" I asked.

"Nope," he said.

"I like you," I said, exasperated, "but you're just not shy enough."

He looked at me with his blue eyes long enough to cause us nearly to sideswipe a parked truck. "You know," he said, "you're not the first person to notice that."

It was a funny kind of evening, but I felt as though it were a real turning point. Now I figured I knew where I was with him. Also, I figured I could handle him. Firm. That was what you had to be with Stu. Also, I realized that the better I knew him, the more I liked him. It didn't make sense because, let's face it, he had ten or twelve major faults, but I liked him.

When I got home and was up in my room, I even hummed to myself as I slid into my ruffled flannel nightgown. "Things are going my way," I sang softly. I clicked my bedroom slipper heels together, pulled back the sheet with a flourish and said, *"Olé!"* Stu's girl, I thought. I could do worse.

My run of good luck was still holding the next day when we had the family conference about working on the house. Dad, who claimed to be impartial, served as chairman and moderator. We held the meeting in the library, practically the only room where you didn't have to step over paint cans. Dad leaned forward in his chair. "Now Kate," he said, "you feel that the house has turned out to be too much to handle by yourself, so you want to renegotiate our initial agreement that it was to be chiefly your project. Is that a fair statement of your position?" Mother agreed that that fairly stated her case. "You, Bitsy," Dad went on, "feel that in order to give your mother any significant help on the house, you would have to cut back on your school or social activities, which you are not willing to do. Is that right?"

I would have liked to have added a few hundred words to that summary about how, by living in squalor in such a weird house, I was making enough of a sacrifice already, but I just nodded my head.

"Let's see if we can find some middle ground," said Dad.

"Mom should hire some teenaged boy to help her," I suggested.

"I don't call that middle ground," said Mom. "We have to consider that in only two years Bitsy herself will be going away to school and we can't be throwing money around."

"Maybe we should sell the house," I suggested brightly.

Dad gave me a look. "I suggest that Kate look into what it would cost to have a teenager help, say, fifteen or so hours a week, and we'll discuss it next week."

"Also, extracurricular activities and good grades may help me win a college scholarship," I went on.

Dad held up a hand. "Meeting adjourned," he said.

It wasn't in the bag, but I felt pretty good. It looked as though the wind were blowing my way. I didn't see it then, but I was counting my chickens a bit too soon. The thing I hadn't realized yet was that you can get every single thing you want, yet have it turn out not to be at all what you had in mind. I don't know how to explain it unless fate has a sense of humor. But of course I didn't know any of that yet.

As we were getting up, Mom said, "There's something else of family interest I'd like to bring up while we're all here. I ran into Martha Brentwood today. I happened to mention our ghost, and she said something very interesting. She said that ghosts are often attracted to houses where people are psychic. Don't you think that's interesting?"

The thing I found interesting was that Mom was trooping all over town telling people about the ghost. And just when I was getting to like being Stu's girl. Just when I was beginning to feel almost like a part of Stu's crowd. I could imagine what they would say about Mom's ghost. They would laugh themselves silly, that's what. Stu would do a killing imitation of Mom. Everyone would make up limericks on the subject. Michael Cowder would pity me. I couldn't stand it. A chill of fear shot through me, but I reminded myself that Mrs. Brentwood probably didn't even know Stu and his bunch. All I had to do was keep Mom from spilling it all out to them herself. That should be simple enough.

"Anyway," Mom went on, "I told her I was sure I wasn't psychic. I can never even find the car keys. But she said she can lend us some of those cards with symbols on them that they use in experiments to see if people have ESP, and she'll show me how to see if you two have any psychic powers. Not that I swallow all that stuff hook, line and sinker, but it doesn't hurt anybody to have an open mind, and I do think it's interesting, don't you?"

"Fascinating," I said with feeling.

4

It was quite a rush getting a dress ready for the Autumn Stomp. I had been over at Mrs. Blitch's getting the final fitting just the night before, and the dance was that night. But Mom couldn't blame Stu for that; after all, we had only known each other two weeks, so it wasn't as if there had even been that much time for advance notice.

I turned slowly in front of my full-length mirror. "What do you think?" I asked Mom anxiously.

"It's beautiful," she said. "Just beautiful."

"Not too tight?" I said.

Since there wasn't too much of me, I thought it was better for my dress to be too tight than too loose. That way it looked as though I'd *planned* to be thin. I had kept telling Mrs. Blitch to make it tighter and tighter, and now I was a little worried I couldn't sit down. I sat down to test it. No problem.

"You know, it turns out that Mrs. Blitch is Toni Alpert's grandmother," I told Mom.

"Did she make Toni's dress, too?" Mom asked.

I sank into gloom. "No," I said. Obviously, Toni would be wearing something very original and glamorous, not something run up by the neighborhood dressmaker. I could imagine her emerging from the Salvation Army thrift shop with something in ostrich plumes and sequins that with a tuck here and there would turn into something wildly terrific.

I looked at myself in the mirror again. Blue. Blue wasn't a very original color. And what could you say about the dress except that it was pretty? When I came to think of it, pretty might not be quite the right effect.

"The dress is perfectly lovely," Mom assured me. "You look great."

"Then why am I so nervous?" I wailed.

Mom smiled. "Maybe it's because you want so much to please," she said.

The doorbell rang downstairs. My stomach felt as if I were going down in an elevator. What was the matter with me?

As I went down the stairs, I could see Stu, his back to me, standing talking to Dad below. He looked tall and cool, the way people look in advertisements, the shirt at the back of his neck so white it seemed almost blue and the back of his head sleek and dark.

I felt a little afraid, as if he were a stranger. But when he heard my step on the stair and turned, I could see it was Stu, after all—freshly shaven and his hair smoothed out but definitely Stu. "Your father's been telling me about his high school days," he said with a mischievous smile at the corners of his mouth.

"So I have," said Dad, looking surprised. "I must have been boring Stu to tears."

Boring him? Not likely, I thought. I'd be willing to bet that he found Dad's fond memories very funny.

I was glad to get out of the house. I was getting a little nervous that if we hung around, Mom might start talking about the ghost and Stu would really have something to chuckle at.

The gym is always tricked out in pumpkins or something like that for the occasion of the Autumn Stomp, and that night bales of hay, skewered with a couple of pitchforks, were stacked at one end of the gym. But at the other end, behind the punch bowl, was the prettiest decoration—autumn leaves seemed to be caught there in midair, as if they had been falling from the ceiling of the gym and had changed their minds and decided to float there in the beam of a red spotlight.

Stu saw me looking in that direction and said, "Toni and her crew did it. They had the devil of a time getting the leaves to stay up there. Managed it with fishing line and masking tape, finally."

"Hey, man!" rumbled a voice behind us. I

jumped and turned to see Harlan. One thing about Harlan, when he loomed over you, you were always relieved to see there was a smile on his face. "You know Susan, Bitsy?" he was rumbling. I saw then that Susan James, the cheerleader, was with him. She was so small it was easy to overlook her. She smiled and clung to Harlan's arm. It's odd how these enormous guys date such tiny girls. What kind of fun could it be for her, staring at Harlan's belt buckle all evening? I noticed that she was licking her lips nervously. It was nice to feel I wasn't the only one on edge.

Stu was standing restlessly, looking out onto the crowded dance floor. He had a way of standing balanced on the balls of his feet as if he were about to take off running. He wanted to dance and led me out onto the dance floor right away. Luckily, I love to dance. Pretty soon I had forgotten about how impressed people would be when they saw I was with Stu, about my dress and about being nervous and was just dancing. A while later, when the music paused, I looked around and was almost surprised to see the people still milling around. Stu's smooth hair had come unsmoothed, and I could have used a comb, too, for that matter, but I didn't care. I shook a strand of hair out of my face, looked at Stu and laughed. He grinned back. People must have thought we were nuts, standing in the middle of the dance floor, laughing.

Just then, who should brush by us but Ronnie and his date. I think it was the first time I had ever seen Ronnie without a pencil over one ear. "Hi, Bitsy," he said dampeningly, as if he had just discovered me shoplifting. I felt sorry for Ronnie's date. She looked like a quiet, easily frightened little thing, mousy in pink tulle. It was clear to me that the girl who dated Ronnie should be made of sterner stuff.

"Hi, Ronnie," I said brightly. "Having fun?"

I don't know why Ronnie always caused me to say such idiotic things. When his black eyes bore into me, my brain seems to go numb.

"I'm covering the dance for the paper," he said, looking Stu over critically.

"Uh, Ronnie, this is Stu Shearin," I said. "Stu, Ronnie Platt, editor of the *Clarion*."

"We've met," said Ronnie coolly.

Seeing how Ronnie was looking at us, Stu put his arm around my shoulder protectively. Ronnie's left eyebrow quivered in indignation. He did not introduce his date. He was no slave to the social niceties. I shot her a small encouraging smile as he led her away. "Have fun, Bitsy," Ronnie said in a nasty tone as they left.

"What's eating him?" said Stu as we started dancing to the slow music.

"I don't know," I said.

Stu looked off in the direction Ronnie and his date were disappearing, and the familiar quirk of a smile began to appear at the corners of his mouth. A lot of people, if they'd been looking at the way Ronnie looked at

Stu, would have wanted to wring Ronnie's neck, but Stu just thought it was funny. "Ronnie's an odd duck," he said.

"Well, he really wants to turn out a good paper," I said apologetically. "He's okay."

Stu was certainly different from Ronnie, I thought. Ronnie liked to make people toe the line and do as he said. Stu just liked to laugh at them. When I thought about it, that was probably what was so attractive about Stu. It wasn't his straight dark brows that I liked or his blue eyes, because even though Stu was a good-looking guy, there were plenty of guys at Riverdale High that were better looking but had never caused a ripple in my world. It was something about the way Stu seemed to be always laughing privately that I liked.

Later on, I danced some with Harlan while Stu danced with Susan. Harlan was so enormous you were surprised he could move at all, but he really could. He had very good rhythm. Then I danced with Dick Morely, Toni's date. Dick was nice, but what I didn't like was that my dancing with Dick meant that Stu was dancing with Toni. I wasn't at all happy about the idea of Toni's floating along the dance floor with her head on Stu's shoulder, although, to be fair, the only time I managed to catch a glimpse of them dancing, they looked as if they could have been talking about the national debt. We met them after that dance at the bales of hay at the end of the gym. It was easy to spot Toni because while everybody else was wearing pretty pinks, blues and soft greens, Toni was wearing a white satin dress splashed with red across one shoulder. The red-splashed shoulder had a long sleeve, while her other shoulder was bare. I would have been afraid that in that outfit I'd look as though I'd been in an automobile accident and bled on my dress, but on Toni it looked good.

"I'll bet Stu is glad to see you, Bitsy," Toni said ruefully as we came up. "I'm no dancer."

Dick took her hand, looked at her with stars in his eyes and said, "Who cares?"

I could have stood for Stu to look at me like that. I had the theory that adoration was good for you, like vitamins. I figured it must make you grow strong and healthy. I would have liked to test my theory personally, but Stu's manner toward me was more what you would call friendly than adoring.

I danced with Michael that night, too. Everybody else in Riverdale danced all evening with the person they came with. It was only Stu's crowd that switched partners among themselves, and since Riverdale isn't a place where people break out of the common mold much, I wasn't surprised to see a couple look at us indignantly when Stu and I switched partners with Michael and Marian. They probably figured what we were doing was practically illegal. It was funny the way they made me feel positively daring when all I was doing was dancing with stodgy, serious Michael.

"How did this ever get started?" I asked Michael while we were dancing. "The switching around between partners, I mean."

The crease between his eyebrows grew deeper as he thought. "I think it must have been Stu's idea," he said finally. "It's the kind of thing Stu likes to do." He thought a minute. "You know, a couple of months ago, we were all sitting around talking about the yearbook." He paused a minute and looked uncomfortable. Maybe he realized suddenly that I wasn't really part of the group. I could already guess what they had been talking about, though. Every year the senior class votes for the best in several categories for the yearbook—best looking, best sense of humor and so forth. I guessed they had been sitting around deciding which of them would get which honor.

"Yes?" I said encouragingly.

"Anyway," Michael went on, "Toni said they should invent a special category for Stu—Most Likely to Make Things Happen." Michael lost his balance then and stepped on my toe, but I managed not to wince. "Of course, it's all a bunch of silliness, anyway," he said, serenely confident of winning "Most Service to the Community."

A few minutes later, I was back dancing with Stu and feeling a little relieved that we had finished with the couple switching. Not only was Stu more fun to dance with than any of the other guys, but he was also just more fun period.

"Was Michael telling you jokes?" Stu grinned, knowing how unlikely that was.

"We were talking about you," I said.

Stu gave me a sharp look and raised one eyebrow. "Well, don't tell me what you were saying," he said, guiding me into a neat turn.

It was getting late in the evening when he looked at his watch. "I want to get away from here pretty soon," he said. "There's something I want to show you over at my house."

I hoped his parents were going to be home. I knew Mom and Dad wouldn't want me to go over there unless I was sure they were, but I didn't feel quite like asking.

"I want to show you the birthday present my parents gave me," he said.

"I didn't know you had a birthday," I said. "When was that? Why didn't you mention it?"

"Yesterday." He shrugged. "I didn't want a lot of carrying on about it."

That didn't sound like Stu. I thought he loved a lot of carrying on. Wasn't he the one who made things happen? But I knew there were still a lot of things about him I didn't understand. I was glad he wanted to show me what he got for his birthday. At least I guessed I was glad. I would have to wait for the final word on that until we pulled up in front of his house and saw whether his parents' car was in the driveway.

We stopped off at the punch bowl before we left. The way Stu and I had been dancing we could have used not just a glass of punch but a shower. Even Stu, who usually looked so cool, was beginning to look damp around the temples. He upended a glass of punch. "It's hot enough in here," he said. "I wonder how many bodies are crammed in this place."

I cast a look at the milling throngs on the dance floor. Just then, a familiar form appeared out of the crowd. It was Andy Lassiter, heading for the punch bowl. When he saw Stu and me standing there, he shied like a horse that had just seen a rattlesnake in his path, but he couldn't very well turn on his heel and retreat, so he came grimly forward. The girl with him caught sight of Stu and smiled, but to my great pleasure, he didn't see her. He was thinking of something else. "Ready to go?" I said to him. He started, then said, "Sure, let's get out of here."

I gave Andy a friendly nod as we passed them. It had been a close call. I certainly wouldn't have wanted to stand at the punch bowl and perform introductions. I could just imagine my saying, "Stu, this is Andy, the guy I really wanted to go out with in the first place, and this is what's-her-name, the girl who snagged him in spite of all I could do." And all the while, I was sure, Andy's girl would be staring at Stu and licking her chops. I was ready to face the perils of going to Stu's house instead.

We were so hot and damp it was a shock to hit the cold night air. I shivered and pulled my wrap around me. Stu was looking up at the sky. "We ought to have the dances out here," he said. "Cool, plenty of room." He felt me shivering and looked down at me. "You're cold," he said in surprise. My teeth chattered in confirmation. I was not cut out for arctic nights. Stu slipped out of his jacket and put it around me. It was still all warm from being around him. I felt a little guilty when I saw the wind blowing against his damp shirt as we walked to the car, but on the other hand, I *was* warm. I just hoped I wasn't going to have it on my conscience when he came down sick.

"Aren't you afraid you're going to catch double pneumonia?" I asked.

"Naw," Stu said.

When we got to the car, I took off his coat and gave it back to him. "Don't you think anything bad will ever happen to you?" I said, a little exasperated.

"Oh, sure, bad things happen to me," he said, surprised. "I just don't catch germs, that's all."

Probably don't stand still long enough, I thought as we roared off through the parking lot.

Stu's house turned out to be just what you would expect, large and handsome. With just a few changes, it could have been a hotel. I saw that there were lights on upstairs, and a shiny station wagon was parked on the street, so the family was at home.

"It's in the garage," he said. I could see that Stu's family had a three-car garage. As we drove up the driveway, the big garage door slowly rose to let us in.

"Goodness!" I said. "I wonder how that works!" Stu looked as if he were about to explain it to me, so I added hastily, "Never mind. I don't really want to know."

He got out of the car and turned on the garage light. Then I could see that besides the little sports car, two other cars were in the garage, a big shiny sedan and a funny-looking old-fashioned black car. The garage smelled faintly of oil and car wax.

Stu patted the black car lovingly on its high, curvy fender. "How about this!" he said. "This is my birthday car."

I got out and walked over to the black car tentatively, not quite sure what I was supposed to say about it.

"It's a real Model T," he said with pride.

I looked at the car with real interest now. I distinctly remembered reading somewhere that Model Ts couldn't go faster than thirty-eight miles an hour, quite a bit less than the speed we usually made in the little sports car. Now that I realized what a slow car it was, it started to take on a certain charm in my eyes. It had a kind of stately dignity, after all. It certainly was shiny for such an old car, and it was a *very* old car. I saw that it even had a crank in front for starting it up.

I imagined us poking along the city streets in it, being able to read the street signs instead of watching them pass in a blur, maybe listening to the birds sing, letting cars pass us for a change. "I guess you'll want to drive this one from now on," I said hopefully.

Stu stroked it gently. "Maybe later, now

and then, just for fun," he said. "I want to be sure to take real good care of it. I wouldn't want it to get wet or anything."

The idea of getting a car you didn't plan to drive was a completely new one to me, and I can't say it struck me as a particularly bright one. I mean, right away it hit me that it was more practical to collect matchbooks than cars. I didn't point that out to Stu, though, because I could tell that on this particular subject he wasn't quite sane.

I hugged myself to keep warm. My enthusiasm for cars, never exactly deep, evaporated pretty quickly when I was standing on the cold cement floor of a garage.

I wondered a little why Stu's parents didn't come out to see what was up. They must have heard us drive up. I knew my parents would have been out to the garage right away to find out why I hadn't come right in. Of course it was possible Stu had told them he would be bringing me by to look at the car; still, it was odd how little Stu's parents showed up. He didn't talk about them much, and I never saw them. Somehow it made them seem far away and unreal.

"Jeez, it's getting late," said Stu, glancing at his watch. "I better get you home." Before we left, though, he carefully swathed the car's nose in a kind of hammock affair for protection, I guess, against whatever dust and damp might lurk in the garage.

"It *would* be fun to drive it," he said, turning the idea over in his mind as we got

71

back into the little red sports car and started to back out of the garage. "But I've got to learn to start it first." I could tell by the growing gleam in his eye that it wouldn't be long before he grabbed the crank and gave it a try.

We were running late by the time we headed toward my house, and Stu tried to make up for lost time by hitting the gas. Luckily, the streets were almost empty, so at least I didn't worry much about our hitting another car or some poor pedestrian. Now if we could just not hit a tree, I thought.

We were speeding down Baker Street doing fifty when I slowly became aware that the streets were not as empty as I had thought. A blinking blue light was coming up behind us. Instead of using its siren in a sleeping neighborhood at midnight, the police car had just turned on its light. I didn't want to be the one to break the bad news to Stu, so I didn't speak, but he saw it himself a minute later and pulled over, tightening his lips.

A police officer in uniform appeared at Stu's window. "May I see your license, please?" he said.

Stu, without a word, handed it over.

I found it kind of scary. In spite of all those books I read as a kid about how the policeman is our friend and although I have never done anything wrong at all, whenever I see one of those blue uniforms, I begin to hear the jail doors clanking in my ears. I found it particularly scary the way the police officer didn't say much. Neither did Stu. He just carefully folded the ticket, put it in his wallet, and we drove away—very, very slowly.

It would have been nice, as we drove the rest of the way to my house, if he had said "phooey" or something, or maybe gone on about how his father was going to kill him, and think of what this would do to his insurance rates. Instead, he said nothing at all. I didn't think of myself as very sensitive to other people's feelings, but I definitely concluded that he was not happy. The old lightness of heart had vanished.

We pulled up in front of my house at a quarter after midnight, and Stu walked me up to the front porch. Dad opened the door.

"Good evening, sir," said Stu politely.

"Good evening," said Dad. "You and Bitsy are going to have to keep a closer watch on the clock next time," he said.

I knew that was Dad's way of reminding me that it was *my* job to see that I got home on time, but the fact was that I hadn't even worn my watch, for it's just a plain stainless steel and leather one that didn't do much for my dress.

"Yes, sir," said Stu.

I waved a little good-bye to him as he turned to go back to his car, and he managed a smile.

I was thinking that if I had been with Andy Lassiter, the atmosphere at the door wouldn't have been so frosty. It was the night of a big dance, after all, and my parents don't usually make a federal case out of fifteen minutes. There was just some-

thing about Stu that made them nervous—
maybe that he was a senior. Or maybe just
that he was Stu and definitely did not strike
you as the type that would win "Most Service
to the Community."

Mom was sitting in the kitchen in her
bathrobe when Dad and I came in. She had
turned on the oven and opened the oven door
to try to warm up the kitchen a little more.
She did not immediately begin her lecture on
responsibility, so I guessed the fifteen minutes was not being counted as a major offense. They were just letting me know not to
make it twenty next time.

"Guess what?" said Mom. "Martha Brentwood came by this evening and brought the
ESP cards. Maybe tomorrow I can test you
two to see if you're psychic."

"That's good," I said. I was still stepping
carefully in hopes of avoiding the responsibility lecture.

"How was the dance?" Dad asked.

"It was great!" I said. "I had a wonderful
time." I waltzed a few steps around the
kitchen table. "A wonderful time!" I repeated.

Mom and Dad didn't exactly look happy for
me. I've noticed this before about parents.
They want you to be happy, but if you're
really, really happy, they start to worry. I
think they have this feeling that if you were
doing everything you were supposed to, you
wouldn't be all *that* happy.

Mom and Dad followed me up the steps to

bed. "The ESP test sounds like fun," I volunteered. Actually, as it turned out, I could have spared Mom the trouble of giving the test. I wasn't psychic; that's for sure. If I had been psychic, I wouldn't have been happy at all that night.

5

On Monday morning, while the newspaper staff room was humming with activity, Ronnie took me aside. "You know I believe in being open and aboveboard," he said. I nodded. Nobody would ever accuse Ronnie of not being blunt. "As you know," he went on, "Allie is leaving at the end of the month, and we'll be without a feature editor."

I looked at him expectantly, like a baby bird about to get a juicy worm.

"You've really carried most of the work of the features for some time," he said.

I nodded again. I knew perfectly well how my life had been all work and no glory. I was anxious for him to get to the good stuff, about how all my hard work was going to be rewarded by his making me feature editor even though I was just a junior.

"And I really was thinking about making you feature editor," he said sadly.

"Are you giving it to Sylvia?" I said, wide-eyed. I could hardly believe that even of Ronnie.

"Sylvia? Are you nuts?" he said. "No, I guess I'll just take it on myself."

"But Ronnie," I said desperately, "it's too much for you to do, being editor-in-chief and feature editor, too."

"I have to think of the good of the *Clarion*," he said. "I've noticed you are going out with Stu Shearin." He held up his hand. "Not that I'd think of interfering in your personal life," he said. "But my past experience tells me—"

For "past experience," read "Sylvia," I thought bitterly.

He went on. "—that when a girl gets caught up in boys and partying, she doesn't always keep up with her responsibilities at the paper."

I was so dumfounded I couldn't think of anything to say. How could he compare a goof-off like Sylvia to someone like me, who has never failed to get her stuff in no matter what? As for getting "caught up in boys," what did he think I was, a geisha girl?

Ronnie, with perfect timing, dropped this on me just before the bell rang, and I had to get on to chemistry class. But what could I do, anyway? I thought, as I stumbled along the hall, pink with fury. It wasn't as if there were a court of appeals for the newspaper staff. And if I rebelled, I knew he was only too capable of making life on the staff miserable for me the rest of the year. Imagine, I thought bitterly, that I had told Stu Ronnie was okay.

Later on, at lunch, Kathleen slipped into the chair next to mine and unpacked her cottage cheese. Although Kathleen has a very nice figure, she had decided to lose weight and was now devoted to cottage cheese.

I poured out my troubles with Ronnie to her.

"That's terrible," she said sympathetically, "just terrible. But did you have a good time at the Autumn Stomp?"

"Kathleen," I said in even tones, "the Autumn Stomp is not the beginning and end of all life. There are things that are more important than the Autumn Stomp."

"You don't have to say that to me," said Kathleen with a sweet, sad expression on her face. "I'm *glad* that you had fun at the dance. You don't have to be worried about my feelings."

Right then I would have loved to take Kathleen and Ronnie both and knocked their heads together.

"You're not eating your lunch," said Kathleen.

"I'm not hungry," I said between clenched teeth.

Kathleen shook her head. "I wish I had that problem," she said, taking a tiny bite of cottage cheese. "I'm going to have to really work at cutting down on what I eat."

"Kathleen," I said, "you look fine the way you are, perfectly fine."

"Then why," said Kathleen with the air of someone producing the unanswerable comeback, "didn't anyone ask me to the Autumn Stomp."

With great self-control, I got up to dump my repulsive lunch in the trash without saying a word. But I heard Kathleen murmur as I left, "I knew she would change when she started going out with Stu."

When I got home from school, I told Mom all about what Ronnie had said. She handed me a paintbrush so I could help out while we talked, but for once she was a lot less maddening to talk to than Kathleen.

"Maybe you should just approach Ronnie directly," she said. "Tell him just what you've told me. Put forth your point of view."

"I don't think it would do any good," I said, gloomily wiping my paintbrush on the edge of the can. "He's so opinionated."

"Marshal your arguments," said Mom. "Make him listen to reason. What do you have to lose?"

"It's early in the year yet," I said. "He could make things pretty hot for me the rest of the year. You should see him light into poor Sylvia."

"You can't let yourself be intimidated by people like that, Bitsy," said Mom, peacefully stroking the woodwork with white paint.

That was easy for her to say. She had never had to deal with Ronnie.

"If you can't reason with him," she went on, "maybe you ought to consider quitting the newspaper staff. It might make him think twice if he knows he's losing a good worker like you," she said.

"No," I said. "Not a chance. Why should I quit something that I'm really good at just because he's giving me a hard time? He's not going to be around forever, you know. He'll graduate at the end of this year, and next year I might even have a shot at editor-in-chief."

"That's the spirit!" said Mom.

"I'll at least get feature editor next year," I said gloomily, "but there's not so much glory in it if you only get it when you're a senior. Anybody can do that."

Mom smiled. She is always saying she's the only one in our family who wouldn't cut your throat to win at Scrabble. Jim and Dad and I are a pretty competitive, ambitious bunch.

"There's nothing wrong with a little ambition," I said.

"Certainly not," said Mom. "And if you feel that way, you have to look at this problem intelligently. Take what you know about Ronnie and figure out what would be the best way to deal with him. It's a psychological problem, really. I'd look at it that way."

I sank into thought. I wondered what would go over with Ronnie. I'd never given too much thought to what went on in that little brain of his. I'd always just tried to stay out of his way.

"What kinds of arguments seem to appeal to him?" Mom went on. "What sort of things get him to change his mind?"

Unfortunately, I couldn't remember a single time Ronnie had ever changed his mind. When I realized that, I got even more depressed.

That evening, Mom and Dad and I ate dinner in the kitchen because we were painting the dining room now. As usual, the kitchen was chilly even though the oven had been on.

"What this place needs is storm windows all around," I said. "That would help cut the drafts."

Mom is always pleased when I show the slightest sign of any interest in the house, so she looked encouraging, but Dad said, "They would have to be made to order because the windows aren't a standard size, and do you have any idea what made-to-order storm windows for a house this size would cost?"

"Oh, well," I said, dishing myself some more mashed potatoes, "maybe we can just stuff bits of paper in the corners the way people did in the old days. Or better yet, we could hang tapestries on the windows and walls the way they did in old-time castles."

Mom took this idea seriously. She can never see a joke if it's about the house. "It's not a bad idea, Eliot. Quilts, maybe. Lots of people hang patchwork quilts on the walls nowadays."

Dad didn't reply. I could tell he had something on his mind because he had absentmindedly been shaking Parmesan cheese on his mashed potatoes. "I had lunch at the club today," he said, "and I ran into Stuart Shearin." That was Stu's father. I was certainly keen to know what he had said that had Dad flinging the Parmesan cheese around so wildly. "He tells me," Dad went on, "that Stu got a speeding ticket coming home from that dance Saturday night."

I shrank into my chair. There was no point in my taking the tack of "I didn't want to worry you." When it comes to something like that, my parents *want* to worry. And if I had known that the episode concerning the ticket was going to come out this way, I sure would have told them. But I didn't.

Dad looked at me. "How fast was he going, Bitsy?"

"I'm not sure," I said uneasily.

"I thought as much," said Dad, as if I had confirmed his worst suspicions. "What's more," he went on grimly, "Stuart tells me that if he gets one more traffic citation, his license will be taken away. That's the kind of record he has."

I looked at Dad wide-eyed. Now I could see why Stu had looked so grim when he got the ticket.

"You should have told us, Bitsy," Dad said, "but I'm not going to moralize about this. It's too important a matter just to talk about. I'm going to take steps to see that it never happens again."

I was holding my breath now.

"I'm not going to forbid you to see Stu,"

Dad said. I exhaled slowly. "But I do forbid you to drive with him," he said. I sat there frozen. What were we expected to do? Go out together on a bicycle built for two in the middle of winter? I was in despair, but I knew better than to say a word. Dad twisted his napkin into a ball. "I am going to buy you an old but reliable car of your own," he said. "You've always said you wanted a car, and now you are going to have one. And every time you go anyplace with Stu, you are going to be in your car, and you are going to be the one driving."

There was a moment of silence while I thought this all out. This was bad, very bad. In fact, it was the end of my social life. How happy Ronnie would be, I thought bitterly. Because one thing I know about Stu—he was not going to allow himself to be carted around in some old rattletrap just for the pleasure of being with me.

After a minute, Mom said tentatively, "Would you care for some chocolate cake, Eliot?"

"I'm not hungry," said Dad, getting up and leaving the table.

I sat at the table with tears streaming down my face. It was all too awful.

"I think your father is being very generous to let you get a car," said Mom firmly. "And I agree with his point of view entirely." She hugged me. "We care too much about our precious girl to let anything happen to her."

"Stu will never go along with this," I said, sobbing.

Mom got up to start clearing the dishes. "If he isn't willing to let you do the driving under these circumstances," said Mom, "then he isn't worth crying over."

I dragged myself up the stairs so I could nurse my misery alone in my room. I supposed I would just see Stu in the far distance now, on his way to class. Maybe he would smile a little in my direction for old time's sake.

I should have seen from the start that it would end this way. After all, I knew how my parents felt about safe driving, and I certainly knew that Stu was driving too fast—no question about that. I felt a sharp pang when I remembered how he had told me to remind him to slow down. It probably wouldn't have made any difference. Fish gotta swim; Stu's gotta speed. But the thing is—I hadn't even tried. I had just sat around like an idiot and waited for my parents to find out. After all, surely I hadn't imagined that Stu could speed all over Riverdale without their ever knowing, had I?

So now I was going to have a car. The irony! Now I had nowhere I wanted to go. Oh, maybe I would visit Kathleen once in a while or go to the library, but that was all. I was sure I wouldn't want to go out for hamburgers or to ball games or movies. I knew that I wouldn't want to go anyplace I might run into Stu with another girl.

Up in my room, I burrowed under my bedcovers and put the pillow over my head. I felt too bad to call Kathleen and tell her about what had happened. I felt too bad to do anything. In fact, the next day, I even stayed home from school.

Mom came to my room the next morning. "Bitsy, didn't you hear me call you?" she said. "You're going to be late if you don't get moving."

I didn't take the pillow off my head. "I'm sick," I said.

In a minute Mom returned with a thermometer and lifted the pillow to stick it in my mouth.

"You don't have a fever," she said a few minutes later.

"That's because my body isn't fighting the germs," I said. "It's just giving in." I put the pillow back over my head.

"You're going to have to tell Stu sooner or later," Mom said.

"Later," I said from under the pillow.

"Well, all right, Bitsy," she said sighing. "Maybe you're coming down with something. But if you're not running a fever by tomorrow, it's off to school you go."

I spent the day reading a five hundred-page novel. I was careful not to drop it on my toe, as I had enough problems already. Mom brought up chicken soup on a tray for lunch. "How are you feeling?" she asked.

"A little stronger," I said.

"Then let's hope tomorrow you're strong enough to face some reality," said Mom.

I couldn't figure out what I was going to say to Stu about Dad's new rule. How would I begin? Of course, looked at one way, it didn't matter what I said to him, since I would never see him again.

At about four, I heard the phone ring, and Mom came into my room again. "It's for you," she said.

I knew by the way she said it that it was Stu. I felt as if I had sandbags on my shoulders. I went into Mom and Dad's room and picked up the phone on their bedside table.

"Hello?" I said hopelessly.

"Bitsy? It's Stu."

It certainly seemed odd to hear the little joking lilt in Stu's voice, doused as I was in gloom and misery.

"I've got some good news and some bad news," he said.

I gulped. All I had was bad news.

"The good news is that I started the Model T," he said, "and the bad news is that it recoiled on me and broke my hand."

"You mean that crank thing in front? It broke your hand?" I said incredulously.

"That's right. It's easy for me to see why they phased out that model, I can tell you. I was cranking the thing up sweet as can be, and the next thing you know, I was in the emergency room getting X-rayed. I'm going to be in a cast for six weeks. I can't hold a pencil, for one thing, but what's worse, I can't even *drive*." He groaned. "I'm going to have to take the bus to school."

I sat up a little straighter on the bed. "You mean it's your *right* hand you broke?"

"You got it. Can you believe that?"

Mom poked her head in the bedroom door

and lifted an inquiring eyebrow. She must have heard the cheerful tone of my voice and wondered what was going on. I smiled stupidly at her. Then I forced myself to straighten my face into sobriety.

"That's terrible," I said to Stu, trying my best to sound sympathetic. "But at least it's nothing serious."

"You're being an awful good sport about it, Bitsy," said Stu sadly. "I don't know how we're going to get together. Meet at the bus stop, probably, with the wind whistling around us, have our parents drop us off at the library so we can whisper together in the kiddie section." He groaned again. "I can't think what it's going to be like not being able to drive. It's unreal."

"Maybe it won't be so bad," I said. Hollow laughter from Stu at the other end of the phone. "The thing is," I said, "my father is going to get me a car." I added hastily, "Nothing new or fancy but transportation, anyway."

The idea seemed to strike Stu as amusing. "I didn't even know you could drive," he said.

"Of course I can drive," I said indignantly. I felt a little uneasy when I remembered the first time I took the driver's test and forgot how to turn on the ignition. "It'll come to you," the examiner had said. But it hadn't. The second time I took the test was hardly a victory, either. The examiner had said, "You may pull out now," and I had pulled out directly into the path of another car. He had said, "I suppose you realize this is the end of the test." I did pass the test on the third try, though. I got 100 percent on the written part, and at least I have never gotten a speeding ticket. I just hoped Stu wasn't going to get me all rattled when I drove with a lot of looks and remarks, because I did need to concentrate. "I haven't had much practice," I told him cautiously. I could hear Stu howling with laughter on the other end. "But I expect you'll be glad to go someplace without being driven by your mother or father," I added sweetly.

That sobered him immediately. "Jeez, yes," he said. "I didn't mean to sound ungrateful, Bitsy. It's like manna from heaven. What a lucky break you're getting a car just when I need a chauffeur. If I had to go and break my hand, I guess it couldn't have worked out better."

I hung up the phone. Mom came in, wiping her hands on her apron.

"Did you tell him?" she asked.

"Not exactly," I admitted. "Stu has broken his right hand," I sang, standing up. "Tra-la!"

"That doesn't strike me as cause to celebrate," said Mom.

I considered that. "Well, it is rotten luck on poor Stu," I said. "And I guess it probably hurt. But you see, it means he can't drive! I'll have to drive him everywhere. He'll be *grateful* for the lift. And he won't get out of the cast until almost Christmas. Six whole weeks!"

Mom did the calculation. "Well, first of December, anyway," she said.

"Ages," I said. "Simply ages and ages."

I knew that Model T was a great car. I had felt a special affinity for it from the beginning. It hit me that it was probably the *deus ex machina* that we learned about in English. That old machine had appeared out of nowhere, clobbered Stu and saved my life.

And obviously I had been right on the button when I thought that Stu would never in ordinary times agree to being driven around by me. You only had to notice the way he laughed when I said I could drive to realize that his point of view on cars and driving wasn't exactly balanced.

That night when Dad came in to supper, he found me singing while I stirred the Hungarian goulash. I have a weakness for Hungarian goulash with good sweet paprika and caraway seeds. I had made some that night to celebrate my good luck.

"Smells good," said Dad, lifting the lid.

I took it off the stove and carried it steaming to the table. Dad lifted his eyebrows inquiringly at Mom.

"Stu broke his hand," she explained to him.

"I may be slow," said Dad, "but I don't see right away why this makes Bitsy so happy."

"He can't drive," I explained.

"So you haven't told him you aren't allowed to ride with him?" Dad inquired slowly. "You know, he'll have to know sooner or later."

"Later," I said. "I choose later."

Dad sat down at the table and spread his napkin in his lap, looking thoughtful. "How long is Stu to be incapacitated?" he asked.

"Six weeks," I said. "Six glorious weeks."

"Hmmm," said Dad.

"I'm really looking forward to getting my car, like you promised," I said, ladling some goulash onto my plate. "Do I go with you to pick it out?"

Dad was still lost in thought.

"Eliot," Mom prodded him, "is Bitsy going with you to pick out the car?"

"Well, if Stu can't drive . . ." he began.

"Daddy, you *promised*," I wailed.

"I did say you could have one," he admitted, looking trapped. "Oh, I don't know. Do you want to go pick it out yourself?"

I thought about it. "Not really," I said. "As long as it gets me there and takes me back and isn't too funny looking."

"All right," he said. "Then I'll pick it out for you."

"When can I have it?" I asked eagerly.

"In the next couple of days, probably," said Dad. "I'll want to have a mechanic look it over first."

"Yummy," I said.

"The goulash or the car?" said Mom.

"Both," I said.

I was feeling so lucky I decided right then and there to confront Ronnie and tell him to make me feature editor or else. After all, what could he do but yell at me? The thought of that made the goulash taste like sawdust in my mouth for a moment, because Ronnie can certainly be nasty when he makes up his mind to be, but I soon gathered up my courage again.

"I think I'm going to tell that Ronnie Platt just what I think of him," I said. "Where does he think he gets off holding it against me that I go to a dance," I said.

"Am I supposed to understand what this is all about?" asked Dad.

"It's a long story, dear," said Mom. "I'm glad you're in such a good mood," she said to me, "because I thought we might work with those ESP cards after supper."

Dad and I looked at each other.

"Did you know that Martha Brentwood's brother is a writer?" Mom said. "It turns out he is writing a book on the haunted houses of North Carolina," Mom went on, "and Martha says he would love to meet our ghost."

"You'll have to be the one to introduce them, Mom," I said, helping myself to some salad. "Dad and I haven't met the thing."

"It may seem funny to you, Bitsy," Mom said, "but Martha's brother is very serious about it. He is going to be in town next month, and we'll have him over then."

"What will you do if the ghost doesn't show up?" I asked.

Mom got up and started clearing dishes away. "If the ghost doesn't show itself," she said, "it will still be interesting to meet Martha's brother. I suppose he'll want to look around the house."

"I hope he's not expecting too much," said

Dad, pushing back his chair to get up, "because it seems to me that we don't have a very substantial ghost."

A smile escaped Mom. "But Eliot, no ghosts are substantial," she said. "That's what makes them ghosts."

"You know what I mean," said Dad irritably.

"You may be right," said Mom, always ready to make peace. "But let's remember," she added, fixing us both with firm looks, "it doesn't hurt anybody to keep an open mind."

After the supper dishes were done, Dad and I had to demonstrate what open minds we had by taking the ESP test for Mom. It was simple enough. She had a stack of cards with symbols on one side, and we were supposed to guess what symbol was on the card by writing it down before she turned it up. If you figured a circle was on the next card to be turned up, you would draw a circle, and so forth. I was happy to see that I was really awful at it.

After Dad had taken the test, too, Mom disappeared in the library to score them. When she finally came out, sometime later, she said, "This is amazing. It really is amazing." She looked at her figures. "You two actually scored quite a bit below chance. Normally, just by sheer luck, a person would have gotten more right than you did." She looked at us with narrowed eyes. "Are you sure," she said, "that you two aren't trying to hide your psychic powers from me."

Dad and I hotly denied it. "If Bitsy and I

feel any psychic powers coming on, you'll be the first to know," he said. "Won't she, Bitsy?"

I nodded vigorously.

Mom sighed. "Well, at least now I can get these cards back to Martha. I've been so afraid I would spill soup on them or something."

She went upstairs to put the cards back in their cardboard box, and Dad said to me, "Let's make a pact, 'Punkin'. If you don't develop psychic powers, I won't, either."

A couple of days after that, Dad brought home my car. It wasn't new—that was for sure—and it had a standard transmission, which I wasn't used to, but it looked as if it were in pretty good shape, all things considered. I knew I should be glad to have it, but there was just one thing that bothered me about it—it was pink. It wasn't just a little bit pink, either. It was really pink. Also, it was big. You don't usually see that much pink at once.

"The mechanic said it was in great shape considering its age," said Dad happily. "He thought I was getting a really good deal on it; in fact, an amazingly good deal."

I thought I could see why he had got such a good deal. Not everybody wants to drive Moby Pink. And I had my doubts about whether Stu would want to ride in it.

Mom and Dad looked at it admiringly. "It looks very clean," said Mom.

"It's been well kept," said Dad.

Amid all this mutual congratulation and preening, it slowly dawned on me that there might be another reason why Mom and Dad liked this car. It was very conspicuous. Wherever it went, people were bound to look at it and notice it. It was definitely not the car to do anything sneaky in. I knew my parents trusted me, but when I saw that car, I suspected there must be somebody they didn't trust. I figured it was Stu.

"Do you think we could give it a paint job?" I asked feebly.

"Certainly not," Dad said heartily. "The paint is in perfect condition. It would be a waste of money."

Oh, well, I told myself. Stu was, after all, disabled. He wasn't in a position to pick and choose. And at least you would never have to remember where you parked, driving such a car. You could just follow the pink glow.

The next afternoon, when I got in from school, I had another little surprise. Mom had hired somebody to help her work on the house at last. As I drove up in the pinkmobile, I saw a teenaged boy working on stripping the thick layers of paint off the balustrades. I pulled the car up in front of the house with a rattle and a jump, having forgotten to shift down when I stopped. He turned toward me, and I saw that it was Andy Lassiter. I gathered my books, opened the door and slid off the high seat to the sidewalk. "Need some help with those books?" Andy called.

Aren't we suddenly helpful, I thought. I guess my dating Stu had caught his attention, after all. "Thanks, I've got them," I said.

Once I got inside the house, I dumped my books on the dining-room table. Mom poked her head out of the kitchen door. "How was school?" she asked.

"Okay," I said, going into the kitchen. She was peeling potatoes over the sink.

"Have you spoken to Ronnie about being feature editor yet?" she asked.

"Not exactly," I said.

Mom raised an eyebrow at me. "Oh?"

"Well, actually, I'm still working myself up to it," I admitted. "Mom, what is Andy Lassiter doing out front?"

"I thought we had agreed that I would hire someone to help me with restoring the house," she said.

"I just wondered how you happened to settle on Andy," I said.

"He's a very solid, dependable, responsible boy," said Mom. She added as an afterthought, "He's also good with his hands. I expect him to be a big help."

Now I knew all I needed to know. Mom was as transparent as cellophane tape. Andy might be very clever with paint remover, but I had more than a strong suspicion he had been hired at least partly so he would be around the house all the time showing how much nicer he was than Stu. Mom and Dad, instead of just sitting around thinking about how much happier they would be if I were going out with Andy instead of Stu, had decided to do something about it. Lots of times I had heard Dad talk at dinner about how unwise this or that parent had been to criticize their daughter's unsatisfactory boy friend. "Drives them together," he always said. So it was no surprise to me that Mom and Dad hadn't criticized Stu in front of me. What was a surprise was that they had planned on a different approach, one I would describe as the "Approach Sneaky."

Of course I didn't say anything about any of this to Mom. I just said noncommittally, "I expect you're right. Andy should be a big help. He's very handy."

As I went upstairs, I thought, Good grief, Handy Andy. It sounds like one of the cards in Old Maid. The fact was that no matter what Mom and Dad thought, I just wasn't interested in Andy anymore, and I doubted that his hanging around the house stripping off paint was going to change that.

6

At lunch the next day, Kathleen asked, "Have you talked to Ronnie yet?"

What was this morbid interest everybody had all of a sudden in my telling off Ronnie?

"Not yet," I said.

"There's no point in putting it off," said Kathleen. "There he is over there right now."

Sure enough, over on the other side of the cafeteria, I could make out Ronnie eating a sandwich while he read a book propped up against his milk carton.

I swallowed hard. "Maybe you're right. It might be a good idea to catch him by surprise." I got up and started inching my way across the cafeteria behind people in folding metal chairs, stepping over dropped pieces of bread and crunching the occasional potato chip under my foot.

When I got over to Ronnie's table, he was so absorbed in his book and his sandwich that he didn't even look up. I sat down across from him. "Ronnie?" I said. He looked up at me, blinking. He was off balance, all right. Now was the time to put it to him. I cleared my throat. "I've been thinking about what you said the other day about me being feature editor, and I don't think what you said makes sense." Ronnie began to look annoyed as he realized that I was criticizing him, but I didn't let him get a word in. "My private life has never interfered with my work at the paper, and it never will," I said forcefully.

Unfortunately, just at that moment, everything went black. Stu had sneaked up behind me and was holding a napkin over my eyes. I let out a little squeak.

"Guess who," he said.

"Stu!" I said, twisting to look behind me. His right hand was encased in a fiberglass cast, so he wasn't in the best shape for playing this kind of peekaboo, but with his left hand and a napkin, he had managed. Trust him to improvise. "What are you doing here?" I squealed. Stu had a different lunch period altogether.

"Some college representatives were visiting today, and it threw my whole schedule out of whack," he said. "Can't wait to see your new car. Is it parked outside now?"

"Yep," I said. "But I can't show it to you

right now. I'm talking to Ronnie about something important."

Stu raised an eyebrow. "Right," he said. "I'll call you after school."

As Stu left us and joined the lunch line, Ronnie said sweetly, "You were saying?"

I could feel the job of feature editor slipping from my grasp. "Look, Ronnie," I said desperately. "Don't you have friends? Don't you like girls?"

I had him there. He was hardly going to sit in the middle of the Riverdale High cafeteria and say that he had no friends and that he didn't like girls. I quickly followed up on my advantage. "But you get your work done. Why should it be any different with me? I'm not like Sylvia. I've never been like Sylvia." I went on resolutely. "I've done good work on the paper, and I deserve a chance to be feature editor. What's more, you know it."

Ronnie began to look hunted. It occurred to me that he wasn't used to being on the receiving end of this kind of thing. "Okay," he snarled finally, picking up his tray to flee. "Okay, you can have your chance. But you'd better be good."

Good old Ronnie. Nasty to the last, I thought as I fought my way back to my table to retrieve my tray. I seemed to have managed not to eat any lunch again. That was no way for me to gain ten pounds. But on the other hand, it did look as though I would be feature editor.

"Well," said Kathleen breathlessly. "I

know I'll be late to class, but I have to know what he said. It looked like smoke was going to come out of his ears any minute."

I flopped down in my chair. "I think I've got it," I said. "I think he said I could be feature editor."

"He did?" said Kathleen in astonishment.

I looked at her in exasperation. "Sometimes I think you don't have any confidence in me at all," I said.

"It's not that," she assured me. "It's just that I *do* know Ronnie." She stuffed her empty milk carton in her brown paper bag. "What did Stu want?" she said.

"Good grief," I said, full of remorse. "I forgot all about Stu. I hope I didn't hurt his feelings, getting rid of him like that."

I remembered how only a few weeks before I had the weird idea that if only I could go out with Stu, my troubles would be over. What a joke! Since I'd met Stu, my life was so full of problems I couldn't even keep track of them all. Then a really awful thought hit me. What if Ronnie was right and I was so busy I couldn't handle being feature editor?

Luckily, I had so many problems, I couldn't brood long about any of them. Right now, for example, I had to give equal time to the question of whether Stu would really call me after school as he had said? I was sure he wasn't used to being treated like so much extra baggage, and I was worried about how he would take it.

That afternoon when I got home, Andy

was already at the house. I could tell because his bicycle was parked out front. Sure enough, I met him as I was going in. He was carrying more steel wool out to the porch. I said hello, but I didn't let it slow me down any. Stu might call any minute, and if he did, I wanted to be near the phone.

"Bitsy?" Mom called from the kitchen.

I went in and dumped my books on the counter. "Why don't you take this tray of hot chocolate and cookies out to Andy for me," she said, handing me a tray complete with doily. "I've put on two cups," she said, "in case you'd like to join him."

"I'd rather stay inside," I said. "I might be getting a phone call."

I did, however, carry the tray out to Andy. He thanked me with a nice smile. "How'd you do on that chemistry test?" he asked.

"Okay, I guess," I said. "I more or less expected most of the questions." I looked at my watch. "Look at the time," I said. "I've got a ton of things to do."

That much was true, but it was also true I wanted to be inside where I could hear the phone ring. Sitting around passing the time of day with Andy didn't have the appeal for me that it once did. I wasn't sure exactly why. But one thing I was sure of—his timing was really off. If he'd said a kind word to me three weeks before, or even two weeks before, I would have been happy to sit at his feet and prattle on about Mr. Hankin's chemistry test until the moon came up. But now, not only did I not much want to, but I really didn't even have the time. After all, on top of chemistry and trig, there was Stu.

I went up to my room and sat down at my desk right away to work on trig, but my mind wasn't really on it. My mind was on the telephone. Luckily, Stu called soon after that. In my headlong rush across the hall to Mom's room to get the phone, I nearly tripped and fell down the stairs.

"Bitsy?" he said. "It's Stu. Do you know how long it takes to get home on that blinking school bus? Thirty blinking minutes, that's how long. I used to make it home in less than five."

Remembering my harrowing rides in the red car, I could believe it. "That's terrible," I said sympathetically. "Tomorrow I'll give you a ride home."

There was a second of silence. "That wasn't a hint," Stu said quietly. "I was just telling you that I just got home, that's all."

"But I'd *like* to give you a ride home," I said. "There's nothing wrong with that, is there?"

"I don't think I'm going to like being driven around," he said.

I decided it would be a good idea to drop the idea of giving him a ride home from school until he was a little more adjusted to the idea of being helpless, but I couldn't resist teasing him a little.

"It'll be good for your character," I said. "A lesson in humility."

"I'm not interested in being humble," he said.

I laughed.

"This is going to take a lot of getting used to," he said sadly. "Look, how about going to a movie Friday night?"

"Sounds good," I said.

There was a pause. "Well, when can you pick me up?" he asked.

"Ooops. I see what you mean. It *will* take some getting used to. What time would be good?"

"How about seven? The movie starts at seven-fifteen."

I had hardly hung up from talking to Stu when the phone rang again. It was Kathleen. "Have you got started on the trig?" she asked.

"Not exactly," I said.

"I need help," wailed Kathleen. "Did you understand what he was saying in class this morning?"

"I think so," I said. A good thing trig had been before lunch when my mind got kind of churned up by all the business with Ronnie. "I'll come on over to your house, and we can work on it together," I said.

It made sense for me to offer to drive over to Kathleen's now that I was a bona fide car owner, but there was one thing I didn't like about it—I was going to have to go out the front door right past Andy and let him give me another warm smile. It was embarrassing. It was an example of the strange way things work out. I had wanted Mom to get somebody to help her with the house, and I had wanted Andy to notice me. Now both my wishes had come true, and it was driving me crazy. But there was no help for it. I gathered up my books and headed toward the door. "I'm going to Kathleen's to do homework," I called to Mom as I passed the kitchen. Then I bravely went out the front door, my head held high.

"Going over to Kathleen's to do some homework?" Andy asked as I passed by him.

"Uh, yes," I said. "How did you know?"

"Heard you telling your mother," he said, grinning.

Honestly, a person didn't have any privacy anymore. I walked down the steps and over to my car, then threw my books on the front seat. "See you later," I called as I got in.

The car started with a little jump and a fizzle because I had forgotten to shift into neutral to start it, but at last I drove away. In the rear-view mirror, I could see Andy standing on the front porch, watching my car drive away. How solid and all-American he looked, I thought. Also, how boring.

Kathleen met me at her front door. "Let's get on to my room in a hurry," she said, "or we'll be roped into blowing up balloons." As we passed through the living room, I saw Mrs. O'Neil sitting cross-legged amid a heap of paper streamers blowing up a balloon. She was pink in the face. Around her, the O'Neil kids were playing cowboys and Indians.

"Pat's having a birthday party at four,"

Kathleen explained. As we passed by, Kathleen said to her mother, "We're going to do trig now," and Mrs. O'Neil nodded, then pulled the balloon out of her mouth, gasping for breath, and quickly knotted it. Patrick jumped right in front of me, blocking my path. "It's my birthday," he said. "Did you bring me a present?"

"Get lost, Pat," said Kathleen, pushing him aside.

We finally made it to Kathleen's room. "Some days," she said, "I'm actually glad I have to come in here to do homework."

"I see what you mean," I said. There was no denying that Kathleen's house had more than its share of noise and confusion.

"The thing that really gets to me," she went on, "is that pretty soon I won't even have my room to myself. Mary Ann is getting too old to room with Pat, so she's going to have to move in with Louise, and that means Janie will have to move in with me."

I agreed it didn't sound good. Janie would probably bring her clothes and shoes to add to Kathleen's already full closet.

"I'm getting crowded out," Kathleen said glumly. "When I go away to college, all the space I've been taking up will be filled up with books and records and knee socks. Then if I want to come home for Christmas, there won't even be a place for me to sleep anymore."

I could faintly hear that the noise level in the living room was starting to pick up. The party must be beginning. "We'd better get down to the trig," I said, "or you'll never make it to college."

Kathleen is not dumb, but she doesn't exactly have a natural aptitude for trig, either, and when we finally finished, we were both pretty wrung out. I could hear the noise of the birthday party still in full swing.

"Maybe I'll go get us a piece of cake," said Kathleen. "We deserve it."

A few minutes later, she came back with cake and milk. "Poor Mom tried to get everybody in the family to go for the idea of one big group birthday party a year," she said, "but nobody was interested."

I propped my legs up on the dressing-table stool and took a bite of the cake. "Guess who my Mom has hired to help her with the house," I said. "Andy Lassiter." I quickly filled Kathleen in on what I saw as my parents' plot to get me to dump Stu and take up with Andy.

"So what?" she said. "I thought you were really keen on Andy."

"Not anymore," I said.

Kathleen sighed. "Just send any extra boys you can't use over here," she said.

"The thing is," I said, "now when I see Andy, I just get ticked off thinking about how he never noticed me until I started going out with Stu. There's something kind of shallow about Andy."

"Are you sure you aren't off Andy just because your parents are throwing him at you?" Kathleen asked.

I thought about it. "I don't think so," I

said. "He's just so boring. And you know the way he knocks things over when he gets rattled?"

"Sure," said Kathleen. "You always thought it was sweet. It used to be your big ambition that Andy would start to knock things over when you walked by, remember?"

I waved that away. That was a long time ago, I thought. "Well, now I ask myself," I said, "if the reason I was so nutty about Andy was that I always felt a little superior to him, if you know what I mean. You have to admit he's a little on the klutzy side."

"I think you've got a bad case of Stu, that's all," said Kathleen.

I sighed and took another bite of cake. "I really do like Stu," I said. "I really do."

"Well, his hand is going to be in the cast for six whole weeks," said Kathleen, "so you've got some time with him left."

Of course, I had told Kathleen about Dad laying down the law on Stu's driving, but I didn't think it was very tactful of her to bring it up now. It made me feel a little cold spot in my stomach just to realize that one of those weeks was almost gone already.

When I went to pick up Stu for the movie Saturday night, I was glad it was already dark. Maybe by the dim light of the street lamp the car wouldn't look so pink. I pulled up in front of the house and hesitated a minute, feeling a little shy about going up to the front door. Stu must have been watching for me, because he came out the door right away. When he caught sight of the car, he stopped short for a second, shielding his eyes. "Help us and save us," he said when he reached me. "This car is running a high fever. You can see how it's all flushed." He poked his head in the window and said with mock concern, "Have you tried aspirin?"

"Get in," I said. "My father picked it out."

"And I always thought your father loved you," he said, opening the door and sliding in on the front seat. He rested his fiberglass-encased hand on the seat beside him. "Now that I think of it," he said, "the pinkness is probably a mark of his affection. You know, as in 'the pink of condition,' 'in the pink,' 'the pink of perfection.'" He looked thoughtful. "I wouldn't be surprised if there's a limerick there somewhere."

"Spare me," I said, starting up the car. Unfortunately, I had forgotten to put it in neutral again, so it leaped forward three feet like a giant pink turtle after a fly, then stopped short.

"Jeez, watch it, Bitsy," Stu said. "I don't want to break the other hand."

"I'm sorry," I said contritely, shifting into neutral. "You're going to have to be careful not to get me confused by making remarks while I'm driving," I said, "because I'm not really used to a standard shift yet."

This time I released the clutch smoothly, and we pulled out into the street in the proper fashion and began moving in the direction of the movie theater.

"You know, Bitsy," Stu said, "I thought this business of not being able to drive was going to be humiliating to me. I thought I was going to feel pain about it every day. I had no idea it was going to be a million laughs."

"Hush," I said. "Oh, I forgot to tell you. Guess who's the new feature editor of the *Clarion*?"

"You," said Stu. "That's terrific."

He sounded like he meant it, too, which was nice. "Do you even know what a feature editor is?" I asked.

"Nope. But I got the idea the other day in the cafeteria that it was something you really wanted to be."

"That's right," I admitted. "I really did. It's not as if the feature editor does such exciting stuff, but what I go for is the glory. I can't wait to see my name right there on the masthead—Bitsy Amerson, feature editor."

Stu shifted his weight and moved his broken hand closer to him.

"Does the hand bother you much?" I asked.

"It's not exactly comfortable," said Stu, "but it's been harder on Dad than on me. You know, the night I did it, he came in on me passed out cold on the garage floor. It was the old 'Speak to me, son. Speak to me' scene."

"No!" I exclaimed. "I didn't know you passed out."

"Jeez, Bitsy, keep your eyes on the road," yelped Stu.

"I'm sorry," I said. "I haven't gotten used to keeping my eyes on the road yet."

Stu passed a hand over his brow. "Jeez," he said.

"You were telling me about when you broke your hand."

"All right. But tell me if it gets too exciting and I'll stop, okay? I want to get there in one piece."

"You were saying you passed out on the garage floor."

"Right. But just for a minute. My hand was pretty much a mess. At first Dad was real relieved I hadn't broken something vital like my back, but once he got over the initial shock and rushed me to the hospital, you could see his mind start spinning with other worries. He made Dr. Oliphant leave in the middle of a dinner party and rush over to meet us at the hospital. Oliphant knew he'd never get another referral from Dad if he didn't make good time. Then the way Dad hovered over him I thought Oliphant was going to have a stroke and be the next one on the table. 'Any tendon involvement, Stan?' Dad would ask. And, 'What do you think the chances are of nerve damage, Stan?'"

"Gee," I said, "you would think with as much blood and gore as your father has seen he would be able to be more calm."

Stu laughed. "Dad's never going to be calm when he thinks he sees my career as a surgeon going down the drain," he said.

"Oh, I see," I said, the light slowly dawning. "The hand."

"Right."

"Stu, when are you going to tell your father you don't want to be a doctor?"

"Not now, that's for sure."

"Why not now?"

"A lot's going on at home," he said vaguely. "Besides," he went on, "why should I spoil the golden years of my youth having pitched battles with Dad. I'm going to wait until I'm away at college and out of his way before I break the news."

"But isn't he likely to break off your funds for college?" I suggested. "Maybe it would be better to get it over with and give him time to quit being mad."

Stu smiled broadly. "Ah, that's where Granddaddy's trust fund comes in. He can't cut off my funds for college."

We pulled up in front of the Riverdale Cinema, and Stu awkwardly opened the door with his left hand. "Now that we've gotten here alive, do I kiss the ground?" he asked.

7

It turned out there were a couple of advantages about my driving Stu around that I hadn't thought about. One, of course, was that I could drive as slowly as I wanted. But the other, which was almost as nice, was that since Stu wasn't coming to my house to pick me up, he didn't have the chance to stand around and talk to Mom and Dad. That meant I could quit worrying about Mom's going on about her ghost or Dad's giving him a lecture on the dangers of speeding. The funny thing was, though, while I was congratulating myself on keeping Stu apart from my parents, he was showing signs of really wanting to see them. He actually went so far as to say, "Maybe we could go over to your house sometime, Bitsy." I ignored it. Usually, if a boy took me to the movie and out to hamburgers a few times, I would ask him over to my house now and then just so I wouldn't feel like a complete leech, but in this case I put all thoughts of that out of my mind. Stu could perfectly well afford to treat me to hamburgers, so why take the chance of letting him talk to Mom and Dad? I was determined to enjoy myself until that fateful day when Stu got his cast off, and I tried not to think farther ahead than that.

Unfortunately, in the middle of the next week, Toni dropped a little bomb in our midst. Stu and I and the rest of the gang were taking advantage of Mamma Carabanini's Wednesday after-school cut-rate special on pizzas and were all crammed into a booth stuffing ourselves when Toni popped her news. "I'm moving," she said. Everyone stopped chewing pizza and looked at her. Of course, people move all the time, but not people in Stu's crowd. They are all kids who've lived in Riverdale their whole lives, kids whose grandparents lived in Riverdale, not the sort of kids whose fathers are transferred in and out by the big companies.

Everyone started to talk at once, but Stu's voice was the only one I heard. "When did you find out?" he asked.

Toni wiped away a tear. "Last night," she said. "It happened so fast I couldn't believe it. Daddy's quit Grandpa's firm and taken a job in New York." She sniffled. "He said he's tired of waiting around for Grandpa to die so he can get promoted. I pleaded with him. I said couldn't he at least wait until school was out? But he said it was a once-in-a-lifetime opportunity."

"Maybe you could move in with me until school is out," Marian said. "I could ask my parents."

"That's really sweet of you, Marian," said Toni, "but I already asked Mom and Dad if I could stay with Aunt Cissy, and they said no. Mom said, 'We're a family, and we're going to move as a family.' I think she's sort of nervous herself about going to New York."

"Unreal," said Harlan woefully.

"I know," said Toni. "It's like it's happening to someone else."

"I wish it were happening to someone else," said Stu.

Then Toni really did cry.

It was bad. I could see that. The middle of your senior year is no time to move to another school. It's really too late to make new friends then. I supposed Toni would just wander about the new school like a lost soul, completely ignored by all the other seniors and wishing she were dead.

One thing for sure—her news certainly cast a pall over after-school fun time at Mamma Carabanini's.

"My family stayed in a hotel in New York once," said Michael, "and at the desk they gave us this handout sheet about how you shouldn't open your door because of muggers."

Toni's sobs gathered steam, and Stu shot Michael a black look. "Of course there's the ballet and opera," Michael added hastily. "Cultural opportunities."

"I've got to pull myself together," Toni sniffled. "It's not the end of the world. I've got to look on the bright side." She blew her nose in a paper napkin. "But right now," she said, "I think I'll go home and take two aspirins."

Michael and Marian slid out to let her out, and we watched her walk out, dabbing at her eyes. Stu jumped up to follow her. "I'll just walk her out to the car," he said. I felt a sharp pain in my heart.

When Stu came back, he was quiet.

"We forgot to ask her when they're moving," Marian said.

"I asked her," said Stu. "Four weeks from today. They're not going to wait for the house to sell."

You wouldn't expect Harlan to be overflowing with sentiment, but he looked as though he might cry.

"Oh, well," said Stu, "come next September, we'll all be splitting up, anyway. Toni's just jumping the gun some."

This depressing thought cast everyone deeper into gloom. It even got me down. Stu made it sound like September was just the day after tomorrow. Then his chin lifted again, and his eyes began to widen a little. "We should have a going-away party for Toni," he said, "the bash to end all bashes." The familiar faint smile began to grow at the corners of his lips. "It can be a surprise.

We'll have a band and all Toni's friends, everybody in Riverdale that she'll want to say good-bye to. Maybe we'll even ask a couple of her old favorite teachers," he said.

"You're talking about a big party," said Michael.

"Nobody's got the room to throw that kind of party," said Harlan. "It'd be different if this were the summer and we could have it outside."

"Bitsy has the room," said Stu.

All eyes turned to me.

"She lives in a gigantic old house," said Stu. "It's even got a ballroom."

"Do you think your parents would go for that kind of idea?" Marian asked me.

I was forced to admit that my parents probably would not mind. Mr. Brandon's men had finished their repairs of the ballroom, and nothing stood in the way of my having a party there.

Stu slapped his left hand on the table. "It's settled, then," he said. "The party will be at Bitsy's."

I should have been glad to see the light come back into Stu's eyes and his smile reappear, but somehow I just felt uneasy, very uneasy.

By the time Stu and I left Mamma Carabanini's, I had eaten enough pizza to kill my appetite for dinner. Besides, I could already imagine Mom happily showing the gang all the quaint features of the house and prattling on about its ghost. Maybe I should have said I was sure my parents wouldn't let me have the party when Marian asked me. Well, now there was no help for it. I would just have to hope for the best.

As we walked out to the car together, Stu put his arm around me. "Don't start worrying about the party, Bitsy," he said. "People worry too much about that kind of thing. Nobody cares what the house looks like or what they eat or drink. People will just be coming to say good-bye to Toni."

I liked having Stu's arm around me. In fact, it was just about my favorite thing in the world to walk along with him close to me, but not that afternoon. I was thinking of how unsure of Stu I was, how I expected every little thing to drive him away. I was afraid of what he would think of my mother, worried about what my father would say to him. And even though I was the one going out with him, I had this sickening fear that he really liked Toni better. I wasn't sure exactly what was going on in my head. Maybe I needed to book an hour with my father in his office and get him to read my mind. But I knew one thing—I was not too happy.

"What's the matter, Bitsy?" Stu said to me once we were in the car. "What's on your mind?" Stu is not dumb, and I guess he figured out that the tears welling up in my eyes weren't about Toni's going-away party. I must have looked pretty pathetic. I didn't say anything at first, but when I put the keys in the ignition, I said sadly, "Stu, do you like me?" I knew that was a dumb and childish thing to say, but I couldn't help myself.

"For pity's sake, Bitsy, put it in neutral," he said sharply. I suppose I must have *really* looked bad then, because he said gently, "Look, kiddo, I like you very much. I really do." Then he ran one finger down my cheek slowly. "It's not something I'd lie about," he said. I looked at him, his straight dark brows serious, for a change, over those blue eyes, and I believed him.

The next day, I went to the library and got out a book called *How to Fix Nearly Everything*. It had a very clear diagram of a toilet tank in it, and with its help I hoped to do away with Mom's mysterious toilet-flushing ghost before the party.

When I got home, I propped the book open on the bathroom sink and lifted the porcelain top off the toilet tank. I peered inside. It didn't look quite like the diagram, somehow, all neat lines and circles. Instead, it looked dark, slightly mossy and full of mysterious bits of rubber, wire and metal bars that weren't in the diagram at all. I fetched a flashlight from the hall closet and tried shining it in the tank. Now I had a weak circle of light shining on the mysterious workings of the thing, but I was no wiser. "This is going to be tougher than I thought," I muttered.

I must have stared at the thing for a good fifteen minutes, first looking at the neat, reasonable diagram and then looking in the tank at all the weird levers and bits of rubber. I came to one conclusion. If a ghost was going to haunt a toilet, it was exactly the kind of weird old toilet it would haunt.

When I went downstairs, I heard Andy arrive. I heard his bike fall with a thud against the house; then I heard the door of the tool house open with a loud creak. I peeked out the kitchen window and saw him carrying a paintbrush and a gallon of paint around front. I hadn't kept track of his work, but I guessed he must have finished stripping the paint off the front porch and was about to start painting it. It hit me that the mystery of the toilet bowl might be child's play to good old Andy. After all, I knew how clever he was with his hands. Maybe when he looked at a lever in a toilet tank, it actually meant something to him. The question was, was I willing to ask for his help? I had to decide fast, because pretty soon he would have paint all over his hands and shoes.

Mom was in the dining room hanging the curtains. I dashed in to her. "Mom," I said breathlessly, "why don't we ask Andy to look at that toilet that keeps flushing? Maybe he can figure out what's wrong with it."

"That's a good idea, dear," said Mom, leaning over to hook the curtain rod onto its bracket. "Why don't you do that?"

"I thought you might ask him, since you hired him and everything."

She looked down at me from where she was standing on the kitchen stool as if I had taken leave of my senses. "Why, Bitsy, you can see that I'm in the middle of hanging curtains. Go ask him yourself. You'd better hurry. I think he's about to start painting the banisters."

I took a deep breath and headed out to the front porch. After all, I didn't see how requesting a person to fix a toilet tank could possibly be seen as a romantic proposition.

Andy was just prying the paint can open when I put the problem to him. The late-afternoon sun was shining slantwise on his neatly combed chestnut hair and his paint-stained sweatshirt. I couldn't help but think how different from Stu he was in every way. Except for the longer, light hairs on his upper lip, Andy's face still ran mostly to peach fuzz, while Stu was already fighting the five o'clock shadow. Andy's eyes were run-of-the-mill brownish, and he was broader at the hip and shorter of leg than Stu was. But it wasn't those differences that mattered when you compared them but something harder to put your finger on. As he stood there patiently listening to me explain the problem with the toilet, it hit me that he could have almost been part of the porch. If he'd been made of blocks of wood, he wouldn't look much different from the way he looked now, standing all brown, clean-cut and calm. It was almost as if he were a different species from Stu, who hummed like a violin string with suppressed energy.

"I just wondered if you could figure out what's wrong with it," I finally finished lamely.

"Sure," he said, stooping to press the top

back on the paint can. "Let me take a look at it."

I led him to the upstairs back bathroom, and he peered into the toilet tank. "Doesn't look quite like the diagram, does it?" he said.

I sighed. "No," I said. "Well, I'll just leave you to it. Let me know if you figure out what's going on."

"You aren't going to keep me company while I fiddle with it?" he asked.

"I don't want to keep you from concentrating," I said.

"You *had* better leave then," he said, turning back to the diagram.

I couldn't believe Andy had made that crack about my being in the room ruining his concentration. The next thing I knew, he would probably be looking at me adoringly. It certainly made me feel uncomfortable. A while later, he came to find me downstairs. "I've checked it and checked it," he said, "and it looks okay to me. I guess I can only say one thing—you've got a haunted toilet." That was not what I wanted to hear.

After Andy got back to his work of painting the banisters, I went in to where Mom was still at work hanging curtains. "Andy couldn't find anything wrong with the thing," I said bitterly.

Mom didn't reply, for she was putting up a new set of brackets and was holding the nails in her mouth.

"I think we should have a plumber look at it," I said.

Mom took the nails out of her mouth. "Why

is it suddenly so important to you, Bitsy?"
she asked.

I explained to her about the party Stu
wanted to have for Toni.

"What a sweet idea," exclaimed Mom.
"The ballroom will be the perfect place for a
party like that. We'll need lots of flowers for a
room that size. I wonder what pots of chrysanthemums will cost. Do you think it's too
early for poinsettias? Of course, the house
isn't all fixed up yet, but I think we can get it
looking pretty presentable. It will be kind of
fun to share the house, don't you think?"

"When do you think we could get the
plumbers out here?" I asked.

"Bitsy, you aren't getting obsessed by that
silly ghost, are you? Just look upon it as one
of the charming quirks of our house. That's
the way I see it." I looked at her meaningful-
ly. "Oh, all right," she said. "Mr. Pacetti is
already coming out Wednesday to put in a
new thermostat in the water heater. I can
have him look at it then."

I could see Mom was getting on a chummy
footing with all the dry-wall men, plumbers,
tile layers and electricians in Riverdale. If
she wanted to meet new people, why didn't
she just join a bridge club like other people's
mothers?

"Wednesday sounds good," I said. "Give
my regards to Mr. Pacetti. I'm counting on
him."

Not surprisingly, on Wednesday afternoon,
Mom reported that Mr. Pacetti thought our
toilet was the funniest thing he had ever

seen, but so far as he could tell, nothing was wrong with it.

I started brooding about it a lot. Sometimes I felt as if the house really were sort of haunted. It wouldn't just lie back and be a house like other people's houses. It acted as if it were alive, as if it were my personal enemy. By now I had gotten to where I wouldn't be surprised if the doors started creaking open by themselves, the windows flew up, and the candle sconces on the walls started waving around like human arms. After all, when a house starts acting like a person, that's what haunted *is*. And it really was getting hard for me to think of the place as just a collection of boards and nails when it was clearly out to get me.

When I saw Kathleen, I filled her in on all the latest complications of my life, but you could tell there was only one of them that really interested her—Andy's sudden attraction to me.

"Maybe you're going to be a *femme fatale*," she said. "You know, one of those women men die for, like Mata Hari."

A few weeks earlier, that would have sounded pretty good to me, but now that I was in the thick of this romance business, I wasn't so sure. "I don't think I'd want men falling for me on that scale," I said, thinking of Andy's stumbling around among the paint cans and looking longingly in my direction. "It's kind of embarrassing."

"I think I could put up with it," said Kathleen dreamily.

"Besides, I don't think I am a *femme fatale*," I said. "Andy would never have looked at me twice if I hadn't started going out with Stu."

"Well, you can't deny that Stu fell for you," said Kathleen.

I rubbed my nose. "I guess I really do think Stu likes me," I admitted.

"Honestly," said Kathleen in exasperation, "are you working full time at feeling inferior or something? Of course Stu likes you. He's been asking you out for weeks."

"Maybe I'm getting nervous about this party we're going to have for Toni," I said. "I certainly do end up thinking about it a lot."

"Oh, it'll be fine," said Kathleen.

8

The day my name appeared on the masthead of the *Clarion* as feature editor, Sylvia quit. That was a good thing all around. Since she had never done much work, anyway, it didn't increase anybody's work load, and it certainly did improve Ronnie's disposition. We had all learned to dread those Monday mornings when he would look at her copy and turn purple in the face.

A couple of weeks later, Mr. Millam, the principal, sent a personal note to the staff room complimenting my article on the problems of students who transfer into Riverdale High in the middle of the year. "Interesting . . . compassionate . . . well written" were a few of the adjectives he used. Mrs. Greenbaum beamed at me. "Bitsy has done such a good job as feature editor," she said.

Ronnie looked modest, as if he had invented me but was too nice a guy to take the credit he deserved. "I knew Bitsy could do it," he said.

I looked at him, speechless.

At home, Andy and Mom continued to make steady progress on repairing the house, but unfortunately there was no longer any doubt that Andy had a crush on me. I started trying to come in the house the back way to avoid him, but Dad didn't like that.

"I don't want you parking your car on Mason Street," Dad said. "That's where my patients park. And you know I want the family to avoid using the back entrance."

"I'm very quiet," I said meekly. "And I haven't run into anybody yet."

"I've spoken my final word on that," said Dad firmly. "That side of the house is the business side, and I no more want the family using it than I would want you hanging the wash in my waiting room."

"Oh, all right," I said. "But I just get so tired of walking past Andy while he looks at me with those adoring cow eyes."

Mom snickered, and Dad gave her a look. "I'm sorry, Eliot," she said, "but I do see what she means." She got up to clear the table. "At any rate, Bitsy," she said, "Andy is going to be working on the hall next week, and then there'll simply be no way to avoid him. You're just going to have to put up with it. After all, he's a good worker, and you've made it clear you don't want to sand the baseboards yourself. Or do you?"

"No," I said, sighing. "I'll put up with it."

Marian had volunteered to do the guest list for Toni's party. She was busy worming out of Toni a complete accounting of everybody in Riverdale she'd ever cared about. It meant a lot of tear-soaked memory-lane sessions after which Marian would rush back to her room and scribble down the names for the invitation list.

Harlan arranged for the band. A friend of his had had one going for about a year, and they weren't too expensive. "They're saving up for a new amplifier," he explained, "and they're glad for any gig they can get." I was hoping that their old amplifier was very feeble and weak, since I wasn't too sure how the house would stand up to any serious vibration.

As the time for the party approached, Mom and I started to clear away the paint cans and sandpaper that were all over the house. Of course, what with all the things like the big floor sander and the wallpaper steamer and so on, we didn't really have room for all of it in the tool shed, so we put up folding screens in the corners of the rooms so we could stash stuff behind them in a temporary way. "I don't know why we didn't think of this before," Mom said. "It'll make the house much more livable while we're doing the restoration."

Harlan and Stu dropped over one day to

see if they could help out, and Stu insisted on writing Mom a check for the flowers as his contribution. He said he thought she ought to let herself go and get both chrysanthemums and poinsettias.

Finally, our united efforts were about to bear fruit. The day of the party had arrived. Mom and I arranged the flowers on the refreshment table and on some pedestals in the corners; then Mom studied the effect. "We need something with more height, I think," she said. "An epergne, maybe. What do you think, Bitsy?"

"I think we have enough flowers," I said. "We don't want this to look like a funeral."

It turned out that Marian's grandmother had a big silver punch bowl we could use, and Marian had brought it over that afternoon. It looked enormous sitting on the damask-covered refreshment table. You had to admit it was impressive.

"I think you could bathe a child in that thing," Dad said thoughtfully.

"Marian's grandfather was governor one time," I explained. "Marian says it was given to him by a grateful citizen."

"I see," said Dad. "Graft and corruption."

Mom stood back and looked at the punch bowl critically. "It needs something," she said. "I'm not sure what."

"A Brink's guard—that's what it needs," said Dad.

"Don't be silly, Eliot," said Mom. "Something that size—you don't need to worry about guests pocketing it."

"What it needs is punch," I said. "When we get the punch and circles of ice in it and pile little sandwiches around it, it won't look so big." Mom and I had spent the previous week making and freezing little sandwiches, and now hundreds of them were stacked in the kitchen.

Dad walked over and poked the fire in the fireplace. Theoretically, the fire was supposed to take the chill off the ballroom. In fact, it seemed to have thrown the thermostat out of whack; if anything, the room was chillier than before, but that didn't worry Mom. "Once people start filling the place up, it'll seem warm enough," she said confidently.

I had to admit that even if the ballroom wasn't toasty warm, it did look great with the punch bowl glowing in the light of the silver candelabra. The flowers made bright splashes of red and white against the damask tablecloth, while above us the crystal chandelier glittered and sent spurs of its light bouncing off the glass of the room's tall windows. It was all glittering and elegant, and to look at it you never would have guessed that downstairs corners of the house were still filled with paint cans, tack rags and scraps of sandpaper.

I heard the front doorbell and jumped. "They can't be here already!" I squeaked. "We haven't got the punch and sandwiches out." We all thundered downstairs in a panic, and while Mom fled to the kitchen to get punch, Dad and I answered the door. It turned out to be the band, and they looked pretty strange. None of the guys actually had a safety pin through his nose, but the effect they gave was the same, with their shiny, tight T-shirts and their strange hair stiff, as if they had let it dry while it was still full of soap. "This the Amerson place?" asked the leader. "We gotta get set up and check out the hookups and the acoustics." The way the guy looked, you were amazed he was capable of human speech, let alone a word like *acoustics*. I noticed Dad was looking at him speechless. "The ballroom is upstairs," I said, turning to lead the way. "Boy," one of them said, looking around as they walked up the spiral staircase, "this place is kind of a period piece, isn't it."

Their boots went clunk-clunk heavily as we walked up. The leader, whose name turned out to be Darryl, took one look at the ballroom and shook his head. "I can tell you right now your acoustics stink," he said, "but what the heck. Most people can't tell the difference." They went in and started looking for electrical outlets. I was willing to bet Marian's grandmother's punch bowl had never had such a disreputable-looking bunch reflected in its plump, curvy sides. I went down to help mother transport punch and sandwiches, while Dad stood protectively near the silver punch bowl. When Mom and I got back with our trays and pitchers, the air was filled with dissonant electrical sounds.

"Is that the music?" Mom asked me anxiously.

"No," I assured her. "They're just getting the equipment set up."

A piercing electrical shriek rent the air, followed by a hollow hum. Darryl called out cheerfully, "Not every day we play under a chandelier, is it, guys?" The other two boys shook their heads in agreement. "Well, you gotta say this place has atmosphere, anyway," Darryl concluded charitably. The other two boys, who seemed to have been struck mute, nodded their heads agreeably.

Once everything was ready, it seemed like eons until the first guest arrived. Stu and Michael showed up together, both of them apparently seized with the fear that maybe they should be there early to help.

"No, everything's under control," I said nervously. "Don't you think people ought to be getting here soon? You do think the invitations got there all right, don't you? It would be awful if Marian had forgotten to mail them."

"Don't be so nervous, Bitsy," said Stu. "It's just a bunch of friends getting together, nothing to get excited about." He cleared his throat. "I did call some people, just to spot check, so I can tell you the invitations did get out."

I looked at him, and he gave a sheepish little smile. "I would hate for there to be any slip-up," he admitted. He glanced at his watch. "Marian should be bringing Toni to

the front door in a half an hour," he said.
"Her story is that she has to stop off at your
place to get a book you borrowed."

Mom started showing Michael around the
house, and Stu followed them, peering into
rooms. "You've done a lot of work since I was
here last," he said. "It's really coming
along."

Mom glowed, although "It's really coming
along" is what I would call an ambiguous
compliment.

Harlan, Susan and Dick Morely showed up
with other guests hot on their heels, and
soon I lost count of who had arrived and who
hadn't. Mom was doing quicky group tours of
the house, and the band had started playing
upstairs. Dad came down looking pleased.
"Nice music," he said. "Funny thing. How
they look doesn't seem to have anything to do
with how they sound."

Not long after, Marian came in the front
door, dragging Toni. Everyone standing
around the front door yelled, "Surprise!" I
didn't know a lot of the people, but Toni
obviously did, because she started to cry. It
was hard to get her upstairs to the party
proper. She wanted to take Mom's tour of the
house. Weird always had appealed to her.
However, even I had to admit the house was
in its glory that night. A party like that was
just what it was made for. Mom had tied
ribbons on the doorknobs, put flowers in the
hall, and with all the people going up and
down the stairs and all over, the place was
full of excitement. Upstairs in the ballroom,

the dancing had started, and as Mom had predicted, the room was turning out to be plenty warm.

I didn't know most of the people, but I stuck to the little islands of people I did know, and what with running up the stairs with refills of sandwiches and punch, I stayed busy. I noticed that Toni had found a footstool and was sitting at the fireplace holding court, with friends stopping by in twos and threes to say their good-byes and to utter words of false cheer about how much she was going to love New York and how they would come see her. I saw her there, her crinkly hair pulled back in a ribbon, with the firelight playing on her, and thought of what a nice girl she was but how I was really glad she was moving away. Just at that point, Stu took his turn to come over and talk to her. I turned on my heel to go for more ice. Stu had, after all, known Toni his whole life. If he had put his arm around her and said something sweet that made her cry, it would only have been what you would expect of an old friend. But I was going to make sure I wasn't there to see it. I didn't want to be reduced to a quivering mass of insecurity the way I had been that day outside Mamma Carabanini's.

"Going to get food again?" Michael asked me as I headed out the door.

I nodded, carefully averting my eyes from the north end of the ballroom where Stu and Toni were sitting.

"I'll go with you," said Michael. As we

walked downstairs, he said, "I've seen how many times you've been up and down carrying those little-bitty sandwiches. Why don't we just carry all the stuff up at one time and leave it in the hall so you don't have to make so many trips. Don't you have some boxes we could stack it in?"

It was a logical idea. I was surprised Mom and I hadn't thought of it. The stretch of hall that extended to the ballroom was chilly enough that no harm could come to sandwiches there. In fact, it was the perfect temperature for preserving ice cubes. Just past the ballroom, the hall terminated in the stairway that led to Daddy's upstairs offices, and the staircase provided an updraft that kept the hall cool. Also, although we hadn't gotten very far in decorating the hall, it did have a longish table in it where sandwiches and punch could be conveniently stacked.

Downstairs, Michael and I dug up some cardboard boxes, stacked little sandwiches in them in layers and carried them upstairs. The punch was more of a problem, but we finally settled on taking a boxful of the ingredients upstairs so that it could be mixed closer to the spot where it was to be drunk. It occurred to me that the new arrangement would leave me more time for mingling with my guests, and since I didn't know most of them, it wasn't entirely a good thing. But then this particular party was for Toni to enjoy, not me. I arranged another trayful of tiny sandwiches and carried them into the ballroom. Michael followed close behind me with two pitchers of punch. At the rate refreshments were disappearing, it looked as though the guests hadn't had a square meal in weeks.

I was only a few steps from the punch bowl when I saw something that made me stop so short that Michael only narrowly escaped crashing into me and dousing me with both pitchers of punch. Stu and Mom were over in a corner near the fireplace, and Mom was telling him something with great animation. Her cheeks, pink with pleasure, almost matched her pretty rose-colored dress, and she was gesturing widely with a cucumber sandwich. Stu, the good listener, his blue eyes guileless, was leaning slightly against the wall, completely at ease. It was perfectly obvious to me that he was enjoying himself very much. He might be fifty feet away, but I knew him well enough to see that he was keeping a firm grip on himself in order to keep from breaking out laughing.

I dropped the tray of sandwiches unceremoniously next to the punch bowl and sailed quickly over to Mom's rescue.

"I've been telling Stu all about the house," she burbled as I came up. "He's been such a patient listener."

I gave him an insincere smile. "Mom, would you like to see the way Michael and I have got the sandwiches and punch set up in the hall? I think it's cold enough out there for them to stay chilled. What do you think?" I took her hand and began to guide her out of Stu's reach. I was happy to be able to put plenty of distance between Mom and Stu, but I was afraid it was too late. If ever anybody had the look of someone being told a dumb ghost story, it had been Stu. Now what I had to do was figure out how to deal with the consequences.

"Oh, I think it's plenty cool out here, Bitsy," Mom said when we got out in the hall and she examined the boxes of sandwiches. "If the punch gets too warm, we can always fetch more ice," she said, "and I'm sure the sandwiches will be fine. It's not as if there's much danger of food poisoning with cucumber sandwiches."

Daddy came out to join us. "I think the party's quite a success, don't you think?" he asked.

"I think so," said Mom happily.

"Maybe I'll just slip up to the office now and catch up on a little paper work," suggested Dad.

Mom gave him a look.

"You mean I don't get to go catch up on my paper work?" he said sadly.

"No," said Mom. "It won't be long before the guests will start looking for us to say their good-byes. I don't want to be stuck saying good-bye to a hundred people single-handedly. Now why don't you go back in and chat with Mrs. Alpert? She's in the midst of moving her entire household and three cats to New York City, and she looks as if she could use a sympathetic ear."

Sometimes on these occasions, Dad will

protest that he listens to people's troubles all day, but that night he obediently headed back to the ballroom. One thing about chandeliers and flowers and silver punch bowls—they do seem to intimidate people into being on their best behavior. I, for example, had a certain temptation to creep up on Stu and trip him, but considering my surroundings, I put it out of my mind. The thing is, I thought, it's all very well to see the funny side of things. I see the funny side of things myself. But I didn't exactly love it that Stu found my family screamingly funny. Of course, I had to admit he hadn't said anything about it to me—not yet.

The party finally began to break up about one A.M. Maybe it was because we finally ran out of sandwiches and punch. Dad and I helped in the business of saying good-bye to everyone. "Lovely party," "Enjoyed myself so much," "Sweet of you . . ." people murmured as they moved out to begin the serious business of claiming their coats.

"I just can't believe you went to all of this trouble for me," said Toni. "It was so sweet of you."

"It was just too kind of you to do this for Toni," agreed Mrs. Alpert. The two of them looked as if they needed not a party but three weeks of rest at a sanatorium. Mr. Alpert had cannily avoided all the fuss by being in New York on business.

"When are the movers coming?" Mom inquired sympathetically.

"Monday, they said," said Mrs. Alpert, "but they wouldn't promise anything. It might be Tuesday."

"I know you'll find New York very interesting," said Dad.

"I'm sure we will," said Mrs. Alpert bravely. "Well, thank you again."

When the last guest had found his coat and departed, my eyes felt as if they were full of ashes. I'm not used to staying up that late. "It was a nice party," Mom said, yawning, "but I'm glad we don't do this sort of thing every day."

I agreed. Privately, I thought I would have been even more glad if we had never done it at all.

9

The odd thing was that the next few days came and went without Stu's saying a word about Mom's ghost, even though he had plenty of chance to. Wednesday night, when the school chorus did a performance of *H.M.S. Pinafore,* the gang gathered together afterward at Mamma Carabanini's for pizza. When I looked around at everybody's faces, dimly lit by the single candle on the table, I thought about how many things had changed since the night a couple of months before that I had squeezed into one of the booths for the first time, feeling outclassed by all Stu's friends. Now I had quit thinking of Michael, Harlan and Marian as famous and important. They were just kids I ran around with. Toni was gone now, and other things had changed, as well. These days, instead of trying to get Andy's attention, as I had tried to do on that first night at Mamma Carabanini's, I was trying to stay out of his way.

"Funny thing," growled Harlan, "I don't feel as squeezed in as usual." He looked around the booth as if he suspected the management of redecorating secretly and disapproved.

"It's because Toni is gone," Michael said.

Stu raised his root beer in a toast. "To Toni," he said. "Let's hope she's happy wherever she is."

Everybody solemnly drank to Toni. I felt a little guilty about being glad she was gone.

"Maybe we can see her sometime if we go up to New York," said Marian. "It would be nice to go there and see some really professional theater."

"What?" said Stu, a smile tugging at the corners of his mouth. "And miss the pleasure of watching little Buttercup trip and fall flat on her face?"

"Poor Ellen," said Marian sympathetically. "Lucky she didn't hurt herself."

Stu looked woefully at his fiberglass-encased hand and said, "Right. I wouldn't wish that on anybody, no matter how they sang."

"I didn't think she was so bad," rumbled Harlan. "Just a little nervous. It was better if you sat up front where you could really hear. She's not real loud."

"Well, I hope Toni does like New York," I said.

"Yep," said Stu, "but you know she's gotta miss one of the big pleasures of small-town life—watching your friends and neighbors make idiots of themselves."

Marian stifled a giggle, and we all looked at her inquiringly. "I was just thinking," she confessed, "of Mrs. Morely, Dick's mother. You know what she's doing for a part-time job now? Advertising for the Chipper Chicken, that new restaurant out at the mall."

Harlan broke into deep guffaws. "I saw her," he said. "She was dressed up like a giant chicken and handing out fliers uptown."

Stu looked at him with wide blue eyes. "I for one think it's wonderful when a mother can find happiness and fulfillment in a career," he said.

Harlan wiped the tears from his eyes and managed to rumble, "Poor Dick. What a scene!"

Stu looked meditatively at the ceiling. "There once was a dear little chickie," he said, then looked at me expectantly.

"Who handed out fliers so icky," I answered readily. I can do limericks in my sleep. But hit by sudden inspiration, Stu finished the limerick himself triumphantly:

"There once was a dear little chickie,
"Who handed out fliers so icky,
"Her son said, 'I'll cry,'
"Her son said, 'I'll die,'

"And he blushed himself sick, sicky Dicky."

Everybody laughed. I had to laugh myself, but I was nervously thinking of Mom and her ghost.

"Everybody looks silly sometimes," I pointed out.

Stu was quick to admit it. "You're right," he said. "And since we know that our turn is going to come, we can giggle at everybody else with a clear conscience, right? Even I can look silly, though you'd hardly believe it."

"Like your being crazy about that Model T," I suggested. "To some people, that might look silly."

"I'll admit it," said Stu amiably. "About that car, I was silly.

"Ah, woe is me, its heart was black.

"I loved that car, and it didn't love back."

"When will you be getting that cast off your hand?" asked Michael.

"Won't be long," said Stu, patting my knee under the table with his good hand. "Then poor Bitsy can quit carting me all over town."

The thought made my heart stop for a second. That's right, I thought. It won't be long. The day of reckoning was almost on me. I had told Dad I would rather tell Stu about the no-driving rule later, but later was almost here, and if anything, I was looking forward to telling him less than when Dad first came down on me. As many worries as Stu had caused me, I couldn't imagine life now without him and his silly limericks. It was too bad I didn't take to Andy, good old, safe, boring Andy, but there it was. Stu was the one I wanted, and things didn't look good.

When I drove Stu home that night, I dropped him off as usual outside his house. I had been picking him up and dropping him off for weeks now and still had seen no sign of his family. If I hadn't known better, I would have begun to suspect that his mother had two heads. I ruled that out, though, because if it had been true, it would have been bound to get around in a small town like Riverdale. Still, it did seem odd that Stu always bounded out his front door before I even got the ignition turned off so I never had to come up to the house. I couldn't help feeling that he was trying to keep me away from his parents. Of course, I had tried to keep him away from my parents, too, but while I had flopped at it, Stu seemed to be having one 100 percent success.

The next afternoon, after school, I went over to Kathleen's just so I would have a shoulder to cry on. By now, her sister had moved into her room, so we went to the Burger Place to get some privacy. It wasn't so much Janie's guitar and record player and knee socks that were making Kathleen's room impossible these days as it was Janie herself, hanging around listening to what we were saying.

Kathleen climbed into my car gratefully. "You can't know how much I want to get out of that house," she said.

Actually, I had a pretty good idea how much she wanted to get out. Now that Andy was always popping out in front of me holding sandpaper or paint cans, I wasn't too keen to hang around my house, either.

"If I can just have some privacy," Kathleen said, "I won't ask for another thing. You wouldn't believe what Janie did to my lipstick. It was so messed up it looked like she'd been eating it."

I deftly turned right. Now that I was used to the car, I could even talk while I changed gears. "Maybe you should lock up your lipstick," I suggested.

"Maybe I should lock up Janie," said Kathleen.

Hardly anybody was at the Burger Place, for three-thirty is not a time most people are driven by hunger to stuff themselves with fast foods. Kathleen and I got a package of cookies to split, then retired to a quiet corner booth to talk. First she told me a good bit about the trials of living with Janie and a little bit about her plans to join the drama club in order to get acquainted with Tom Durren. I listened attentively. It was only fair that she get equal time. But I was happy when we got down to talking about what was really on my mind—Stu.

"Stu's cast is going to be coming off any day," I told her, "and you know what that means."

"When exactly is it coming off?" said Kathleen, munching a cookie.

"I'm not sure when his doctor's appointment is," I said. "I guess they'll probably have to X-ray to make sure it's mended properly." Then a cheerful thought struck me. "Of course, maybe it won't be mended and they'll have to leave it on a while longer."

"You don't want Stu's hand to be permanently crippled just so he'll keep going out with you, do you?" said Kathleen.

"Oh, no," I said hastily. "But if it were *slow* to mend . . ." I sighed. "It was just a thought."

"Anyway," said Kathleen, "what makes you so sure Stu will drop you when he finds out you'll have to keep doing the driving?"

"You don't know how crazy about driving Stu is," I said. "And he thinks he's a good driver. He's going to think Dad is being really unreasonable."

"That's not your fault," Kathleen said.

"Also," I went on, "I wouldn't call Stu the worst macho case I've ever seen, but I don't think he gets a big thrill out of me picking him up at his house. I think he has the idea that it's in the nature of things that boys do the picking up and driving."

"But if he really likes you . . ." said Kathleen.

"I'm not sure he likes me *that* much," I said. "I mean, who would spend their whole senior year being chauffeured around in the pinkmobile if they could help it? And, after all, nobody's indispensable. Look how fast Toni disappeared without a trace. Everybody thinks it's too bad, but nobody sits around crying into their root beer." I thought for a minute about how roomy the booth at Mamma Carabanini's was going to be after I was gone.

"Don't look so upset," Kathleen said. "Think of all the things you've overcome already this year. Remember how much you wanted your mom to get somebody to help restore the house? Well, she got somebody, didn't she?"

That was a poor example of overcoming something, I thought. It was more a matter of out of the frying pan and into the fire.

"Then think how you took on Ronnie!" Kathleen went on. She had been really impressed by that. "Now you're feature editor!"

I had to admit that was some consolation. When Stu dropped me, at least I would have something to be besides Stu's ex-girl. I would bury myself in my work. I would be a career woman.

"Quit looking so tragic," Kathleen commanded me. "You'll find something to do with yourself if Stu drops out of your life."

I sighed. "I know," I said. "But one thing I am not going to do is go out with Andy Lassiter. I'd rather sit home with a good book."

Kathleen shot me a warning look, and I saw that Andy was bearing down on us, tray in hand.

"What a surprise to run into you here!" he said blandly.

Not likely. With my giant pink car parked out front, my being inside couldn't be less of a surprise if they'd been blaring on loud-speakers that I was making a personal appearance.

"Hi, Kathy," he said offhandedly to Kathleen. She hates to be called Kathy. I could see she was coming around to my point of view about Andy already. He sat down beside us and smiled at me, pretending that Kathleen was invisible. "Looks like you're going to ace chemistry, doesn't it?" he said to me.

"I've been lucky," I said, not feeling it necessary to mention the hours I'd spent slaving over the textbook.

"And they say smart girls aren't cute," he said, looking soulfully into my eyes.

The way Kathleen hates to be called Kathy, that's how I hate to be called "cute." I may not be six feet tall, but I like to think I have some human dignity.

"I'm afraid we've got to run, Andy," said Kathleen, doing a passable job of looking truly regretful. "I promised my mother I'd cook dinner tonight."

I stood up quickly and smiled at him. "See you later," I said. He stood aside to let us by, and we tore out of the place as fast as we decently could.

As we were driving home, Kathleen said, "I think I see what you mean about Andy. He talks to you like you're three years old. You know, as if you're not quite a real person yet. Funny I've never noticed that about him before."

"Love brings out the worst in lots of people," I observed.

"I wouldn't call that love," said Kathleen disdainfully. "He acted like you were a possum he'd treed."

I had to admit Andy did have a way of making you feel cornered.

"Now see what I mean about not wanting to be Mata Hari?" I said.

"I doubt if Mata Hari had to put up with that kind of stuff," said Kathleen. "She probably carried a knife." But I could see that the encounter with Andy had given Kathleen food for thought. Maybe now she'd have a better idea of what it was like for me to meet those soulful eyes at every turn.

Back at my house, preparations were growing intense for the approaching visit of Mrs. Brentwood's writer-brother. It had long before been decided that the proper entertainment for Malcolm Brentwood was a séance. He suggested it himself. He said that having one would increase the chance that our ghost would show itself, and he and Mom had been writing letters back and forth for the past month, discussing the best conditions for the séance.

"A small room is best, Malcolm thinks," Mom said one night at supper, reading from his latest letter, "because of the more intimate atmosphere, but that's all right because all along I've planned to use the library. Luckily, it gets dark so early this time of year we won't need heavy curtains. We need a table, but that will be easy. We'll just put the card table in there and cover it with a tablecloth. That's really all there is to it. It should be fun."

Dad and I didn't say anything, so Mom looked at us both and said, "Open minds, remember?"

"I don't see why I have to be there," grumbled Dad.

"Do you really want Bitsy and me to entertain this loopy author all by ourselves?" said Mom sweetly.

"I'll be there." Dad sighed.

"I'd appreciate it, Mom," I said uncomfortably, "if you wouldn't mention the séance to Stu if you run into him." I felt bad saying anything at all about it, because I didn't want it to seem as if I were ashamed of Mom, but I couldn't stand it anymore.

"But I already have," said Mom in surprise. "We talked about it the night of the party. Stu said he had read about séances and that they were generally much the way Malcolm proposed we have ours." She folded Mr. Brentwood's letter and put it back in the envelope. "Whatever else you might say about Stu," said Mom, leaving the impression that she could say plenty if she let herself go, "he's a good listener and very intelligent. I found his comments on séances quite interesting."

"You couldn't be starting to like Stu, could you?" I asked.

Mom looked at me wide-eyed. "Why, Bitsy,

I've never said I didn't like Stu. He's always seemed like a very pleasant young man to me."

Right, I thought. That's why Andy was dragooned into being the handyman around here—because you were so crazy about Stu. But I had things on my mind other than my parents' unsuccessful attempts to manage my love life. I knew now for sure that Mom had spilled all to Stu on the night of the party, down to the refreshments to be served on séance night. The big question was Why hadn't Stu cracked any jokes about it? Could it be that he had more tact than I'd been giving him credit for? Or could it be that he'd been reading about séances because he actually believed in ghosts?

10

Friday, the night of the séance, Mom was almost as nervous as she'd been when we threw the big party for Toni the weekend before. "At least the house is in order," she said. "Things are still put away from when we cleaned up for the big party. Of course, it looked nicer then, when we had all the flowers. Do you think we should go out and get flowers?"

"No," I said, "I don't." I realized that poor Mom was anxious for Mr. Brentwood to think we had a nice house. She was used to Dad and me criticizing the house, but it would be demoralizing for her if someone like Mr. Brentwood, who really understood and liked old houses, turned up his nose at it.

I was in a funny kind of mood. I almost

hoped that the ghost would show itself so Mom's séance would be a success. Most of all, I felt bad that I'd been embarrassed about Mom and her ghost and her old house. After all, who was more important to me—Stu or my family?

"Where are you going, Bitsy?" asked Mom in surprise when I headed out the door. "It'll only be a couple of hours until Malcolm and Martha arrive, and we've got to eat supper before then."

"I'm just going out for a minute to run an errand," I said. "I'll be right back."

What I did was to drive to the florist's shop. I intended to blow my allowance on flowers for Mom. Once at the shop, I made my way through hanging baskets of ferns and past floral arrangements that featured baby shoes to the desk. "May I help you?" asked the slender young man who was arranging carnations in a vase.

"I'd like some . . . uh, flowers," I said. I had to give him credit for not smiling, since it's hard to see what else you could buy in a florist's.

"What sort of thing do you have in mind?" he asked.

I couldn't very well ask for something for a séance, so I just said lamely, "Chrysanthemums."

"We have some very nice chrysanthemums over here," he said, leading the way to some horrible, bristling bronze-colored ones. I'm not crazy about flowers from the florist. I know they aren't really artificial, but they look as if they were. I'd rather have a few bug holes in flowers and have them actually look as if they had once grown in the ground. But I finally decided on some yellow ones that cost twenty dollars. Since they were a guilt offering, I didn't want them to be too cheap. I knew that once I handed over my month's allowance on the flowers, my guilt would shrink by leaps and bounds, and sure enough, no sooner did I part with my money, than I began to feel a lot better.

Out in the car, I propped them carefully on the floor of the back seat and drove home. Mom was astonished when I walked in the door with the potful of chrysanthemums. "I thought you said we didn't need flowers," she said.

"I don't think we do really," I said, "but these are a present for you because you think we do."

Mom hugged me. "That's so sweet, Bitsy," she said.

I felt so good I wondered why I wasn't this kind and thoughtful all the time.

Mom was jumpy all during supper. It was hard for her to believe everything was really ready. "We haven't forgotten anything, have we?" she said, looking at Dad appealingly.

"The library has been set up for the séance a full week," Dad said in long-suffering tones. "Of course everything is ready. The only thing you might need to do is go around and dust everything because it's been sitting around being ready so long."

"I've already done that," said Mom. "I ran

the feather duster over everything this morning." She jumped up to look in the refrigerator at the stuffed pastries she was going to offer the Brentwoods with their coffee. "I do hope I made enough of these things," she said, staring at them.

"The man is a writer," Dad said, "not a long-distance runner. You should be glad I went into psychology and not the diplomatic corps. What would you do if you had to entertain the Maharajah of Whatnot week after week?"

"Have a nervous collapse," said Mom honestly.

"The diplomatic service—that would be fun," I said thoughtfully, helping myself to some carrots. "People parking their camels in the driveway, assassination threats, mystery, adventure. Too bad you didn't go into that, Dad."

"There's enough excitement for your mother and me right here in Riverdale," he said firmly.

"Everybody finished eating?" said Mom hopefully.

"No," said Dad.

"I hope you aren't going to take all night," said Mom. "I want to get these dishes cleared away."

"I feel the need to fortify myself against the experience," said Dad, helping himself to more rice. I realized I was probably the calmest person at the table. Mom and Dad were both on edge.

I went with them to answer the door when

Mr. Brentwood arrived with his sister short-ly after supper. He was a small bald man, neatly dressed in a three-piece suit. Miss Brentwood was small, like her brother, and they both had the same pointy nose.

"Come in, come in," said Dad heartily.

They carefully wiped their feet on the mat and came into the hall. "What a charming house," said Mr. Brentwood. "Quite unusu-al."

"Would you like me to show you around?" said Mom.

"Dear me, that would be a treat," said Mr. Brentwood. "Wouldn't it, Martha?"

"Oh, yes," said Miss Brentwood. "How kind of you. Malcolm is so interested in old houses."

While Mom and Dad gave them the full tour of the house, I carried the coffee service into the drawing room. Usually, when my parents have guests for dinner, they pour the coffee right out of the percolator, but Mom had figured the Brentwoods were the sort of people who were less interested in how hot the coffee was than in how prettily it was served, so Dad had polished grandmother's coffee service for the occasion. I waited while they took the tour of the house. Then, when I heard their steps coming down the staircase, I swiftly poured the coffee from the percolator into the plump silver coffeepot and ran back to the kitchen to stash the percolator. A second later, panting, I was running back from the kitchen with a pol-ished silver tray filled with warm pastries and laid them down with a gentle clunk on the coffee table. I think it is the only way to manage using a silver service when you don't have two footmen and a parlormaid. At least it was the only way I could think of to be sure the coffee would still be hot and the pastries at least warm when they walked in. I just had time to slip into a chair and was demurely crossing my ankles when they came into the room. "A rare privilege," Mr. Brentwood was murmuring to Mother. "I would be so interested to hear more about your research on the Moran house." Mom sat down and looked at the silver service uncertainly. I suppose she had last used it at my christening and would have liked to consult the instruction pamphlet. "Coffee, Martha? Malcolm?" she asked. Both the Brentwoods allowed as how they could stand some coffee, so Mom picked up the coffeepot gingerly and began to pour it out into grandmother's treacherous cups. They are very pretty, but it's hard to know which goal their designer achieved more efficiently—that of cooling off the coffee instantly with their graceful funnel shapes or that of adding excitement to otherwise boring tea parties by their tendency to tip over. "Charming cups," cooed Mr. Brentwood. "Heirlooms, I suppose." Mom modestly assented. I was beginning to see why she was so nervous about the Brentwoods coming. They weren't the kind of guest you meet at the door with an invitation to join you for hot dogs in the rumpus room. Luckily, though, they didn't expect me to do anything but look neatly dressed and keep quiet.

When the ceremony of the coffee was finished and we all went into the library for the séance, even I began to get a bit nervous. I couldn't decide what would be worse, for the ghost actually to show itself and scare me to death or for it not to show itself and guarantee that the evening would be a social flop. "The room is perfect," Mr. Brentwood assured Mom. "Intimate, charming. I hope the spirit will favor us with its presence here."

Our chairs were around the card table, which was spread with a tablecloth that fell to the floor and disguised its telltale humble steel-tube legs. We sat down while Dad got up and turned off the lights. Then we all held hands, resting our elbows on the table. I had Miss Brentwood's hand—dry and papery —and Mom's, which was damp in the palms from nerves. It was dark in the room but not absolutely pitch black. I suppose some light from outside was leaking in around the curtains, because after my eyes got over the initial shock of the lights being out, I got to where I could just make out the forms of the other people around the table.

"We must all try to be in a receptive frame of mind," said Mr. Brentwood softly. "Relax. Open your heart to the spirit world . . ." He had hardly got the words out of his mouth when the spirit world made itself known in no uncertain terms by giving the card table a shake. It was an eerie sensation to feel the table give that little jump. I had no idea things happened that fast in a séance. Mr. Brentwood let out an involuntary squeak of delight, then everyone was suddenly very quiet.

When I started thinking about it, I decided that somebody had moved the table with his foot. I looked suspiciously over in Mr. Brentwood's direction but could only make out the faint roundness of his bald head. Then, suddenly, the table jumped again. It was as if someone were trying to pull it away from us. I heard Dad say, "Well, I'll be darned," in a puzzled sort of way.

"Oooh, this is very good!" said Mr. Brentwood. "The spirits seldom come forth so quickly. I wonder if this spirit has something important to tell us." He called in a wavering voice, "Spirit? Are you trying to tell us something, spirit?"

This time I felt a cold draft on my cheek. "Did you feel that?" I whispered.

"What?" said Dad.

"The cold draft," I said.

"I felt it," Mom said.

"Hush," said Mr. Brentwood, his voice trembling with excitement. "Let's see if we can encourage the spirit to speak to us. O spirit, do you have something to say to us?"

Miss Brentwood twittered, "I felt it. I felt it. The spirit is here. I know it."

"I'm sure the spirit would speak," said Mr. Brentwood agitatedly, "if we were all in a properly receptive state of mind. Now let's relax and open our minds to the spirit world. Be receptive! Open your minds!"

I could hardly believe that I, a reasonable person in the twentieth century, was sitting here waiting for a spirit to speak, but I tried to do my part by being receptive. It occurred to me that if the spirit did in fact make an appearance, maybe I could tell him to buzz off for good. That might annoy Mr. Brentwood, but I'd bet it would stop the silly toilet from flushing.

"Open your minds," murmured Mr. Brentwood. "Relax . . ."

When I tried to do as he said, I began to notice the warmth of Mom's and Miss Brentwood's hands in mine, the faint cloth texture of the tablecloth under our hands, things that had been there all along but that I just didn't tune in to until I started to try to relax. There was the whiff of a familiar fragrance in the darkness, too. I couldn't quite place it.

"Open your mind," murmured Mr. Brentwood monotonously.

Suddenly, a strange metallic voice said, "Greetings."

I jumped. We all jumped. The séance had hit pay dirt, no doubt about it. Then, suddenly, I remembered where I had smelled that scent before. It was Stu's aftershave lotion! Without thinking, I jumped up from my seat, almost knocking the frail card table down, and rushed to the light switch. "Bitsy!" Mom exclaimed. "What are you doing?" In a flash, while everyone was still blinking in the sudden light, I headed for the folding screen we had put in the corner of the room to hide odds and ends of the restoration. Before I had even reached it, however, there was a scuffling sound behind it, and it came crashing down, almost bringing the card table with it. And behind it sat Stu, looking sheepishly up at me and surrounded with all the things he had needed to be a first-class ghost—a pair of old-fashioned bellows for making cold drafts, a shepherd's crook for tugging at the legs of card tables and a kazoo for the ghost's strange voice. I noticed that the cast was off his right hand. He had lost no time making use of his new mobility.

"Well, I never!" spluttered Mr. Brentwood.

"I wouldn't have thought you capable of this kind of childish joke, Kate," said Miss Brentwood, gathering up her purse indignantly and moving toward the door.

"But I didn't know about it," said Mom plaintively as they stormed out.

The Brentwoods were more spry than I thought. They were out of the house before we had even completely realized what was going on, and I heard their car leave with an angry roar and a backfire.

Dad was laughing. In fact, when I looked at him, he was wiping tears away from his eyes. "Honestly, for a minute there," he said, "I was beginning to wonder if I was going to have to revise all my ideas about ghosts."

Mom sat down. "I don't think I'll ever be able to convince Martha Brentwood that I didn't plan all this," she said. She looked at Stu reprovingly.

"Those two don't have much sense of humor," Stu said sheepishly.

"Most people don't," Dad said, "when the joke is on them."

I looked at Stu.

"Well, it was funny, Bitsy," he said in his defense.

"It was funny," I agreed, "but it wasn't very kind."

"I didn't expect to get caught," Stu said. "It was just a private little practical joke. I'm sorry it turned out to be so embarrassing for you, Mrs. Amerson."

From the look on Dad's face, I could tell he was envisioning the whole debacle again. "Well, Stu," he said, "I can understand the temptation. I have to say I can."

Mom put her hand to her forehead and managed a smile. "My farewell performance at a séance," she said. "From now on, I don't want so much as a ouija board in the house. Now I think I'm going to go lie down for a while. Good night, Stu."

I walked Stu out to his car, which he had cunningly parked back on Mason Street where it wouldn't be seen. "I think Mom and Dad are being awfully good sports about it," I said. "After all, it was pretty mortifying for them."

"You don't have to rub it in," Stu said. "I'm sorry. Do you think maybe I should send flowers to your mom?"

"I think it would be better just to look humble and apologetic every time you see her for the next ten years," I said.

"Okay," said Stu, climbing into the little red car. "I guess I can manage that."

"I don't think so," I said.

After he drove off, I walked, shivering, back through the front door, latching it behind me as I always do, and a thought struck me. Stu's prank was so spectacular that I was only just now giving any thought to how he had managed it, but now I asked myself, How had he gotten in the house?

The next morning at breakfast Mom was her cheerful self again. "Everybody should have one most embarrassing moment," she claimed. "Now, no matter how bad things get, I can always say to myself, at least it's not as bad as that awful séance."

I felt pretty guilty. After all, I was the one who had loosed the plague of Stu on the household, and nobody was even throwing it up to me, which made me feel even worse.

"About that toilet," Mom said, buttering her toast. "I have already called Mr. Pacetti about it. I'm going to have the whole thing torn out and have him put in a new space-age version that will behave itself."

"Sounds good," said Dad, looking up from the morning paper. He folded the paper up, then rose to put on his jacket. Saturday was usually a busy day for Dad at the office. "Only two appointments this morning," he said, "but later on, Patsy is coming in to help me catch up on the paper work." He started to leave, but as he reached the kitchen door, he turned back to say casually, "I noticed that Stu has his hand out of the cast."

I rested my chin on my hand. "That's

right," I admitted. I wished I had the same simple feelings toward Stu as my parents did. From their point of view, life would just be more restful with Stu out of the picture. For me, it wasn't that easy. I wasn't blind to Stu's faults. If I had been, a night like last night would have ripped the blinders from my eyes. It was just that for me the things I liked about him were more important than the things that now and then drove me crazy.

I got up to help Mom put the breakfast dishes in the dishwasher; then, when she went out to run errands, I drifted aimlessly upstairs. I had some reading to do for American history, but I had a hard time concentrating on it. In fact, I was so preoccupied with my own thoughts that when I came down to the kitchen to get some hot chocolate later in the morning, I wasn't watching my step and ran smack into Andy, who was painting the kitchen door. I had known he was supposed to paint the kitchen doors that day. A little more careful thought and I would have skipped cocoa or gone out to a snack shop for it.

"Hi," I said tepidly, taking the cocoa down from the pantry shelf.

He put down his paintbrush and followed me into the kitchen. "I was wondering," he said, "if you might like to go to the Christmas dance with me?"

I looked up, startled. The honest answer to the question was "No, I wouldn't." Instead, I said, "I thought you knew I'd probably be going with Stu." I felt a little pang in my heart as I said it, realizing that it was by no means certain, but after all, Andy didn't have to know that.

He grinned. "I thought that business at the séance last night would have cooked Stu's goose," he said. "Your mother was telling my mother about it this morning."

I wondered why I had never noticed before how smug Andy looked. "Stu's sense of humor does run away with him sometimes," I said slowly, "but he doesn't mean any harm. He's really a kind person."

I didn't trust myself to stand peacefully stirring cocoa while Andy grinned smugly at me, so I turned on my heel and left the kitchen through the other door and fled the house in my car. As I drove away, I thought that at least Stu wasn't all caught up in surfaces the way Andy was. Stu was really interested in people, even if he did spend a lot of time laughing at them. He wasn't in the habit of talking to me as if I were his pet bunny rabbit, either.

I'm not usually the sort of person who broods. What with one thing and another, I am busy doing something most of the time and don't spend hours looking at the moon and thinking about the meaning of life. But today I brooded. I drove around in the car a long time, going by Riverdale's town square, by my old grade school and then the high school, thinking all the time about life. Then I went out to the shopping mall, where a person can loiter without being conspicuous, and stared sightlessly into shop windows. I tried to be mad at Stu for his silly practical joke, but it was hard to put my heart into it. In fact, now more than before, I realized that I just liked Stu too much to stay mad at him. It was hard to face that I was going to have to learn to get along without him, but the cast was off his hand now, and I was going to have to tell him about Dad's verdict on his driving.

When I got home, it was lunch time, and there was no sign of Andy. While I was congratulating myself on this, I saw that Dad, who was sitting at the kitchen table, looked pretty upset.

"What did the police say?" Mom was asking him.

"What's going on?" I asked, pulling up a chair at the table.

Mom and Dad looked at each other. Then Dad said to me, "Now, Bitsy, this is to go no further, understand? This is to be kept strictly quiet."

I nodded.

"My office has been burglarized."

"The typewriter?" I asked. I knew Dad had just bought a whiz-bang electric typewriter that did everything but talk.

"Not the typewriter," said Dad heavily, "the files."

"The files?" I said. "What would anybody want with those?"

"I hate to think," said Dad.

"Some ill-informed person might think they contained information that could be used in blackmail," Mom explained to me.

"I'm very careful about what I put on paper," Dad groaned, "but as many people as I see, I have to record a certain minimum amount of information so I can keep the facts of the case straight."

"And someone took all the files?" I asked.

"Not all of them," Dad said, "just some random handfuls. It makes me think they must have been after something in particular. They only took several handfuls so it wouldn't be so obvious which particular folder they were after."

"What did the police say?" Mom asked again.

"They're sending someone around," Dad said.

Just at that moment, there was a knock at the back door. Dad rose wearily to meet the police. As he turned to go, I chirped, "Gee, I guess you're right. We *do* have enough excitement in Riverdale without you joining the diplomatic corps." Dad gave me an unfriendly look as he disappeared. I guessed he was not in the mood for cheerful comments.

After he left, I said to Mom, "Are you sure Patsy didn't take some of the folders home to work on?"

"For one thing," said Mom, "Dad would never let Patsy take the folders out of the office. For another thing, he double-checked with her just to be sure before he called the police."

"I wonder how long they've been missing," I said.

"It's hard to be sure," said Mom. "If your father hadn't been looking for a particular folder this morning, he wouldn't have known anything was wrong until he needed one that turned up missing. He called Patsy right away, and she came over here to check the folders against her filing list so they would have a clear idea of what was gone. Then they called the police."

"It certainly is weird that they didn't take the typewriter," I said.

"Do you want some lunch, Bitsy?" Mom asked. "I don't think your father is going to be eating for a while."

"Maybe I'll fix myself a grilled cheese sandwich," I said, getting up. Of course, the whole thing was awful for poor Dad, but for me it was nice to have something else to think about besides the everlasting problem of Stu. I got the cheese and butter out of the refrigerator. "Seriously, Mom," I said, "don't you wonder why they didn't take that new typewriter?"

"Not really," she said. "It's heavy and bulky, and obviously they just weren't after that kind of thing. What I wonder about is how they got in."

I was spreading my bread with butter, but I stopped short when she said that. It sounded so much like an echo of what I had been saying to myself the night before after the séance fiasco. How did he get in? I began to get a very cold feeling at the bottom of my stomach, but I forced myself to keep on slowly spreading butter over the bread. "You mean they didn't break in the front door?" I asked casually.

"No, they didn't," said Mom, "not as far as your father can tell, and of course the windows are kept locked all during the winter, so it doesn't seem they could have come in that way."

I carefully arranged cheese slices on a piece of bread, topped it with another buttered slice and put the sandwich in the skillet. "How could they have gotten in, then?" I asked. My voice sounded odd to me, but Mom didn't notice anything.

"That's what your father and I were asking ourselves just before you came in," said Mom. "As you know, the door to the office at the top of the inside staircase isn't kept locked, so it would be fairly easy for someone to get into Dad's office from our house. We were trying to go over who had been in the house, and you'd be surprised how many people have—the plumbers, the pest-control men, the dry-wall men, Andy, and then only last weekend we had that big party with the band and a hundred people, hardly any of whom we knew personally." Mom sighed. "It's simply amazing how many people you can get suspicious of once you start."

I stared as if hypnotized at the sandwich sizzling in the skillet. The cheese was oozing out of the simmering sandwich, giving off the sharp smell of cheddar, but my appetite had vanished. What possible motive could Stu have for stealing Dad's files? The idea that he might want to blackmail somebody was laughable. Wasn't it? But it was undeniable that Stu had gotten into the house the night of the séance, so I supposed he could get in any time he wanted. That didn't seem to have occurred to Mom and Dad. Maybe they thought I had let him in to set up his prank. But I knew I hadn't.

"Isn't that sandwich burning?" Mom asked, sniffing at the air.

I whipped it out of the skillet hastily. It had definitely gotten rather carbonized around the edges while my mind was on other things.

Dad talked to the police for quite a while that afternoon. Then he and Patsy spent some time trying to narrow down the field of suspects, checking her dictation reels to see if an entry had been made in one of the missing folders since the big party. Unfortunately, Patsy had spent a lot of the past week dealing with typewriter salesmen and had fallen behind on her regular dictation, so she hadn't made many entries into case folders.

At supper that night, Dad was feeling very low. "The thing I'm wondering," he said, "is when should I tell my patients that they can expect a call from the local blackmailer any minute."

I could see why he was depressed. It was hard enough to get people to come in even when they weren't afraid details of their personal life might show up in the newspaper. Dad heaved a sigh and wearily pushed his food to the other side of his plate.

"Maybe the police will catch the culprit so soon you won't need to tell anyone," Mom put in.

Dad looked at her so morosely that she decided not to try to make another optimistic comment and got up to get dessert instead. Of course, none of us were hungry for dessert.

By the time I went to bed that night, I knew I was going to have to find out how Stu had gotten in the house, and I was going to have to find out soon, before Dad and I both went crazy.

11

The next afternoon, I drove over to the house of Adam Winter, the cabinetmaker. It was Sunday, but I could hear the power saw running in the workshop behind his house, so I went ahead and walked on back to the shop. I stood at the door for a minute, waiting for him to notice me. Thin winter sun was pouring through the bare windows of the shop onto the gleaming metal of the shop machinery and the curly wood shavings on the floor.

When he switched the saw off, he saw me standing at the door and nodded slightly. I wasn't surprised that he didn't speak, because while he was working on our secret cabinet, I had learned he was a man of few words. He was maybe in his thirties with close-cut nut-brown hair and a mild way of looking at you as if he found you rather more puzzling than a cabinet.

"Mr. Winter," I said, "do you remember me? I'm Bitsy Amerson. I want to ask you a few questions about that secret cabinet in our house."

He didn't exactly answer but looked attentive, like a very intelligent gerbil, so I went on.

"What I'm wondering," I said, "is whether there is any way a person could get into the house that way."

He thought about it, then gave me a slight nod.

"There is?" I asked. "Do you know how it works?"

After a pause, he finally nodded again.

I realized there was no point in asking him why he hadn't mentioned it. It was perfectly plain that he never mentioned anything unless you dragged it out of him with pliers. "Has anybody else asked you this but me?" I asked suddenly.

His face lit up. "Stu," he said. "Stu Shearin. Now he's really interested in how things work."

For Mr. Winter, it was quite a long sentence, and I guessed Stu's charm had something to do with it. I imagined him spending lazy hours hanging around Mr. Winter's workshop staring at wood shavings and waiting for him to come across with the information needed to break into our house.

"How does it work?" I asked.

He looked at me dubiously, as if wondering

whether I had the intelligence to understand an explanation even if he could have been able to bring himself to make one.

"Let me put that another way," I said patiently. "I mean, if I wanted to get in that secret way, where would I go?"

"Trap door in the tool shed," he said, looking surprised, as if the answer were obvious.

"Do you mean," I said, almost unable to believe it, "that I could go through a trap door in the tool shed and actually end up in our library?"

"Don't," Mr. Winter advised. "Old. Not safe." He turned back to his saw to indicate that the interview was now over and then added as a second thought, "And mice." Then the saw burst forth with a roaring whir, and I jumped back.

I left the workshop and climbed back in my car, feeling a little dizzy with all I had learned. I still wasn't sure exactly how the secret entrance worked, and I wasn't tempted to try it out, particularly after hearing about the mice, but now I had found out what I needed to know. I knew that Stu had discovered how it worked. And though I had no proof, I was sure he had gotten into the house that way. The only question left was whether he had stolen Dad's files. And why? What possible reason could he have had?

I suppose there were a lot of things I could have done then. I could have gone to the police. I could have gone to Mom and Dad. I could have just sat tight and felt awful. Instead, I drove without hesitating straight to Stu's house, parked my car out front and walked up the front walk. As long as I had been coming to pick up Stu, I had never gone up the front walk before, and I felt kind of funny about it. I was sure his parents would think it was strange that I had showed up unannounced on Sunday afternoon. Still, as uncomfortable as that might make me feel, I realized it was as uncomfortable as I would feel just sitting around all afternoon thinking about what I'd found out, so I walked up to the door and rang the doorbell firmly.

I heard Stu yell, "I'll get it." In a second, he had whipped open the door and was standing before me, restlessly balanced on his toes in that way he has.

"Bitsy!" he exclaimed. "What's up?"

"I need to talk to you," I said.

"Sure. Just a minute. Let me tell Mom I'm going out," he said, turning on his heel and charging up the stairs in the hall.

For a minute, I wondered if maybe he was going to climb out on the roof and make a getaway the way people do in movies. But a second later, he was tearing down the steps toward me, his blue eyes so clear and unquestioning that I wondered if he knew what I had come to talk to him about.

"What's on your mind?" he asked, climbing into the car.

"Let's wait until we get somewhere we can park," I said. I was a lot more confident about my driving now, but I knew this was one conversation I wasn't going to be able to manage and drive at the same time. In fact,

I wasn't sure I was going to be able to manage it at all.

After we parked in the lot of the Burger Place, Stu turned sideways, leaning against the car door, and waited for me to speak, calmer than I had ever seen him, his eyes resting quietly on me. When I looked at him, it was hard to believe he could ever do anything dishonest, and I couldn't bring myself to come right out and accuse him. I bit my lip and looked out the windshield.

"Stu," I began, shrinking from the main point, "there's something I've been keeping from you. After that night you got the speeding ticket, the night of the dance, my father told me he wouldn't let me ride with you anymore. That's why he got me this car, so that any time we went anywhere together, I could do the driving. You see, even now that you can drive again, if we go anywhere together, I would still have to do the driving."

I didn't think he really took in what I was saying. "Did you hear what I said?" I asked him.

"It doesn't matter," he said. "Look, Bitsy, there's something I've been keeping from you, too. In fact, there's so much I've been keeping from you it's hard to know where to start."

I felt a cold clutching in my stomach. He was going to confess. "You stole those files from Dad's office, didn't you?" I said.

He hesitated a minute, then said, "Yes. But I've sent them back. I put them in the mail this morning." The familiar smile started at the corners of his mouth. "No return address, naturally."

"Why?" I cried. "What earthly reason could you have for doing it?"

"My brother—Brian," he said uncomfortably, "he's been having some problems. In fact, he's been seeing your father."

"Those files are private," I said hotly. "Taking them is a criminal offense. Dad has called the police."

"I had to know what was going on," he said. "You don't know what it's like around my house, Bitsy. I might as well be living behind the Iron Curtain for all the information I get. Brian has been going around shrieking and banging his head on the wall, and Mom and Dad have been dropping hints about him going to live away from home, and he's only thirteen. And nobody will tell me anything about what's going on. Nobody would tell me what was the matter or whether things would get better or whether I would ever see him again or anything." He went on bitterly. "I guess I'm just not supposed to notice that things are falling apart. Sara and I are supposed to waltz on as if nothing is going wrong and show everybody what a great family we are. You can't imagine what it's been like."

He was right. I couldn't imagine it. If that was the way Stu's family was, no wonder poor Brian was beating his head against the wall. People have to be able to talk about what's bothering them. I still didn't like what Stu had done, but I was sort of beginning to get an inkling of why he had done it.

He leaned back again against the car door. "It turns out Brian isn't nuts," he said. "At least that seems to be what your father thinks. I found that out from the folder. Dad is just driving the kid bonkers. And all the time, when I thought they were sending him away to some weird hospital or something, they were actually just planning to send him to boarding school next term to get him away from Dad."

"I'm not sure I really understand what's going on," I said hesitantly.

"Well, you know what my father's like. All he ever thinks about for us is good grades and medical school. He can't help himself. Even if he doesn't *say* anything, you know what he's hoping and expecting. I just sit back and laugh at the whole thing, but poor Brian's having a rougher go of it."

"I guess you were relieved to find out nothing was really wrong with Brian," I said.

"I feel like a different person," said Stu luxuriously. "You would think Mom and Dad could have said a few words to me about what's going on, wouldn't you? I mean, it's not so horrible. And now that I'm not worried sick, I can't believe I've been doing all this cloak and dagger stuff. It looks kind of silly, if you see what I mean. I knew I just wanted to tell you the whole story and quit having secrets. But it turns out you knew, anyway."

"Stu, did you read any of those other folders?" Of course, he had no right even to read Brian's folder, but somehow to read the others seemed to me far worse.

"I swear, Bitsy, I put them in a large manila envelope addressed to your Dad and mailed them back without peeking at a one." The quirk of a smile appeared at the corner of his mouth. "Used surgical gloves for the whole operation, natch. No fingerprints."

"It's just hard for me to picture," I said slowly, "that you came tiptoeing through our house some night when we were asleep and burglarized Dad's office."

Stu winced. "I wish you wouldn't use the word burglarize. Think of my feelings. That's what I did, though. And talk about jumpy! I was a wreck. I could just picture the scene if your Dad caught me pussyfooting in the hall at two A.M.!"

"Lucky we're all good sleepers," I said sweetly.

"Look, Bitsy, I know it was a rotten thing to do. I'm just trying to make you see why I did it, that's all. And you have to see that the secret door was a big temptation to me. The minute I saw that cabinet of Judge Moran's, I thought there must be some way to get in and out of the house through there. And it turned out there was. The cabinet just lifts right out, and zip you've got the door. Of course, it took me weeks to get that out of Winter the cabinetmaker. And once I tried using the thing, I could see why he didn't advertise it. It's really crumbling. When I was coming through the little tunnel, some bricks fell down, and all these little critters scurried out of my way. Yech."

"The night of the séance, you came in that way, didn't you?" I asked.

"Yep. My idea all along was to create confusion about who could have taken the folders, you see. Toni's big party was a help because the house was full of strangers, but I thought it would be even better if people started thinking maybe the ghost had whisked the folders away. That's why I tried to play up the idea of the ghost the night of the séance. But then that didn't come off exactly smoothly. How did you guess, anyway?"

"Smelled your aftershave lotion," I said.

Stu fingered his jaw. "I'll have to keep that in mind if I go in for a life of crime," he said.

"You've just been telling me," I said sweetly, "that you *have* gone in for a life of crime."

"Aw, give me a break, Bitsy. I told you I didn't read the other folders and that I've sent them back. Don't you believe me?"

I thought about it a minute. "Yes, I believe you," I said slowly. "I guess what really upsets me is that now I see that all the time you were using me to get at those files." I hesitated a minute, then repeated sadly, "All the time."

When I thought about it, I didn't feel mad anymore. I just felt sad and awful. Kathleen had been right. It had been strange that Stu had asked me out. Now I knew what his real reason had been.

"Look, Bitsy," he said seriously, "I want you to believe this. It's the truth. That was the reason to start with, but then things changed."

I looked at him, wanting to believe him.

"Remember that first day I gave you a ride home?" Stu went on.

Of course, I did. But it seemed like years earlier, when I was young and trusting.

"Remember how I didn't have much to say?" he asked. "Well, have you ever known me to be at a loss for words since?" he asked.

I thought about that, and as I replayed that scene in my mind, the little red car, the awkward exchanges, I realized there was something to what he said. If I had known him then as I knew him now, I would have known Stu wasn't acting like himself.

"I had never gone in much for deceit before," he said sheepishly, "and I wasn't sure I could go through with it. But then, when I started getting to know you, I really took to you."

"Convenient," I said.

He reached out and put his hand on my knee. "Come on, Bitsy," he said, "give me a break."

When I looked down, his poor hand, so freshly out of the cast, looked white and a little wrinkled, as if it had been underwater. I covered it with both my own. What a mess this all was! I liked Stu so much, but everything was such a mess!

"You're going to have to tell Dad," I said.

He winced. "You think so? I guess you're right. I shouldn't let him suspect everybody else in creation. But I'm not looking forward to it."

"You don't know the half of it," I said with feeling. "He is really upset. I mean really, really upset. And you can take it from me that he's not going to be able to see the funny side of it." Gradually, I became conscious that we were parked at the Burger Place. I supposed I had driven there planning to get something to eat. "Do you want anything to eat?" I asked.

Stu craned his neck to look at the drive-through menu posted behind us. "I think I could stuff down an apple turnover and a tall milk," he said.

In spite of myself, I could feel my appetite coming back. An apple turnover sounded pretty good. I backed up and pulled into the drive-through lane to put in our order.

"You know," said Stu, "as soon as I got my hands on that folder, I could feel my sense of proportion oozing back. Up till then, all I thought about was how I could find out what I wanted to know. But once I found it out, I couldn't *believe* I had actually been crawling through that tunnel at two A.M. and tiptoeing through your house to get it. It was crazy."

I shuddered, thinking of the falling bricks in the tunnel. "You could have been killed," I said. "Nobody would even have known what happened to you."

"Now you're really giving me the creeps," said Stu. "I guess the first thing your Dad will do is padlock that trap door."

"No," I said. "The first thing he'll do is yell at you until you wish you could crawl into it again."

I turned to give our order to the speaker. "Two apple turnovers, two large milks. That's all, thank you," I said.

"Thankyouverymuch," garbled the metallic voice of the speaker. "That will be two dollars and fifty cents. Please pull up to the drive-through window. Thankyouforcoming to the Burger Place. Haveaveryniceday."

I have noticed before that how polite people are is in inverse proportion to how much they really care about you. The voice in the drive-through speaker fell all over itself wishing me a happy day, but it really didn't care if I lived or died as long as I remembered to pick up my change. I pulled slowly along the line toward the drive-through window.

"Look, Bitsy," Stu said seriously, "you do believe me? What I said?"

The fact is, I did. That's why I was getting my appetite back. When people really care about you, I think you usually know it. I don't know how, but you know. And if I needed proof, hadn't I heard with my own ears Stu the car nut saying it didn't matter that I was going to have to drive him around in the pinkmobile all year? I guess I had been uncertain about Stu before because somehow I had had the feeling he was hiding things from me. But now he was saying what he was really thinking, and I knew it. "Sure, I believe you," I said peacefully.

After we got our turnovers, I pulled over into a parking space to eat them. Of course, we could have gone inside if we had wanted everything we said to each other to be repeated all over Riverdale, but we decided it would be smarter to put up with the chilly car.

"It's really kind of cold," I said, shivering. "Maybe I should have gotten hot chocolate instead."

Now that Stu had two good hands, he could put one arm around me and still not abandon his grip on his turnover. He nuzzled my cheek, and I felt him warm next to me. It was a nice feeling, but a sigh escaped me when I thought about what a pickle we were in.

A little later, while we were driving back to my house, an unpleasant thought struck Stu. "You don't think your father is going to forbid me to see you altogether when he finds out I lifted the folders, do you?"

"I don't think so," I said. "Dad is absolutely convinced that forbidding people to see each other drives them closer together. This is going to be the acid test, though, of how much he believes his own theory, because he is *not* going to be happy with you."

The afternoon light was starting to fail, and as we drove up to my house, it looked all peaceful and mellow in the long red rays of the setting sun. Silly old house, I thought. You and your dumb secrets and your wretched ghosts, causing nothing but trouble. But I guess I realized then that I was getting kind of fond of the place. You couldn't say it was boring.

As we came through the kitchen door, we found Mom and Dad at the table, Dad with his head in his hands, looking thoroughly low. They looked up as we walked in, and I said, "Dad, Stu needs to talk to you about something."

Stu was embarrassed. "Privately," he added.

Dad looked absolutely terrified. I realized he must have thought that Stu was coming to ask for my hand in marriage or something. Of course, that was good in a way. It meant that when Stu came out with his confession, Dad might be positively relieved. It might keep him from strangling Stu on the spot.

They disappeared together into the library, and I quietly filled Mom in on what was going on. She didn't say anything at first, probably following her own rule of "If you can't say anything nice, don't say anything at all."

"Stu's been under a lot of pressure, Mom," I said. "It's not the sort of thing he would normally do."

"I hope not, Bitsy," she said flatly. "If he made a habit of it, he could end up in a cell at the state penitentiary." She got up to stir a pot, and after a few seconds, sounding a little softer, she said, "Of course, all of us have done things we've regretted at one time or another. And I have to give Stu credit for deciding to confess to your father."

It seemed as if Stu and Dad were in the library for an awfully long time, but at least I didn't hear the sound of thudding bodies within. Finally, they came out. Stu gave me an uncomfortable look, and I guessed it was as close as I was ever going to get to seeing him look humble. Dad managed a little half smile and started up the stairs. Then Stu and I went out and got in the car to head back to his house. Stu slumped in the seat and held his hand to his forehead. "This hasn't been the best week of my life," he said.

"Was he really mad?"

Stu thought about it. "Not exactly mad. I think he was relieved to find out exactly where those folders were. But he wasn't going to nominate me for the Good Citizen of the Year Award, that's for sure." Stu shifted restlessly in his seat. "Look, Bitsy," he said, "you're not feeling kind of generally fed up with me, are you? I mean, wishing to see the dust from my heels and so on?"

I grinned at him. "No."

He groaned. "I can think of times I've felt like a better deal."

"That's just a little humility you're suffering from," I said. "I expect you didn't recognize the feeling at first, but don't worry, it'll go away pretty soon."

"Come on," he said, "don't tease me. I feel awful."

"Nobody's perfect," I said.

Just then, Harlan's car passed by us, going in the opposite direction. Harlan beat a quick rooty-toot-toot on his horn, did a U-turn in the middle of Elm Street and pulled up behind us. I pulled over, and Harlan bounded out of his car over to ours, followed reluctantly by a little brunette who was every bit as tall as the average eight-year-old. She was bundled up in a big, fuzzy lavender sweater that made her look even smaller. Harlan leaned on Stu's window and said, "We just came from visiting Billy Ann's brand-new baby brother at the hospital, and we're on the way to Mamma Carabanini's to celebrate the big event. Want to come?"

Billy Ann murmured to me, "I wish Harlan wouldn't go around telling everybody. It's kind of embarrassing."

"I don't think we'd better," said Stu to Harlan. "Bitsy and I have already been to the Burger Place, and I've got to be getting home."

As we drove off, Stu said to me, "Where does Harlan find these midgets? Think how many girls he must have to interview before he comes up with one short enough to suit him. It tires me out just to think of it." He reached over and gently pushed my hair back behind my ears, and I smiled at him. "Now if he just stuck with one funny girl, the way I do," he said, "think how much happier he'd be." His eyes widened a little. "Wait a minute," he said, "I feel a limerick coming on." He closed his eyes and finally came out with:

> Confessing to one of his dumber tricks,
> Stu said in dismay, I am in a fix.
> Now I feel two feet high,
> There is mud in my eye,
> But I still have my Bitsy and limericks.

He grinned.

"You're hopeless," I said affectionately. He didn't deny it.

Genuine Silhouette sterling silver bookmark for only $15.95!

What a beautiful way to hold your place in your current romance! This genuine sterling silver bookmark, with the distinctive Silhouette symbol in elegant black, measures 1½" long and 1" wide. It makes a beautiful gift for yourself, and for every romantic you know! And, at only $15.95 each, including all postage and handling charges, you'll want to order several now, while supplies last.

Send your name and address with check or money order for $15.95 per bookmark ordered to
Simon & Schuster Enterprises
120 Brighton Rd., P.O. Box 5020
Clifton, N.J. 07012
Attn: Bookmark

Bookmarks can be ordered pre-paid only. No charges will be accepted. Please allow 4-6 weeks for delivery.

N.Y. State Residents
Please Add Sales Tax